The Happy Eating Approach

Buddhist advice on happy eating for optimal health and weight

by Tara Springett

Copyright by Tara Springett 2015

All rights reserved

ISBN-13: 978-1516888719

ISBN-10: 1516888715

Contents

Acknowledgements 4

Introduction
Buddhist wisdom for a happier approach to food
and weight issues 5

Enjoyable step one
Eat when you are hungry 25

Enjoyable step two
Eat natural food 61

Enjoyable step three
Eat only what you really feel like eating 93

Enjoyable step four
Eat as much as you enjoy 124

Enjoyable step five
Love yourself and others 145

Sample page for a food diary 175

About the author 176

Acknowledgements

I want to give a heartfelt "thank you" to all my clients for trying and usually succeeding with the happy eating approach. Also, I want to say a big "thank you" to my husband Nigel who patiently went along with all the many improvements to our diet I made over the years. He lost 16 kgs of weight and is now at the same weight as he was as a teenager. A special "thank you" goes to my son Jamie for always eating what I put in front of him without too much protest and for helping me with the cover of this book.

Introduction
Buddhist wisdom for a happier approach to food and weight issues

There are thousands of books about diet and healthy eating on the market and they all promise health and weight loss. The most astonishing and also confusing fact is that many of these books are totally contradictory. One approach urges the reader to cut out fat, the other says exactly the opposite – eat lots of fat but cut out the carbohydrates. Other forms of diet dictate that we should or shouldn't eat dairy and meat with the same force of argument; that we should or shouldn't have three or six meals a day and that raw food is either wonderfully good for us or will lie half-digested and rotting in our intestines and will make us ill over time.

If we combined all these diets into one single food plan virtually *everything* would be forbidden. This confusing situation begs the question – just how is it possible that all these experts have come up with such a mess? Even though you will always find a number of people who swear by the most extreme diets, you will also always find many other people who say the exact opposite and claim that the same diet didn't help them at all. Obviously, there must be a factor that different diets work for different people.

But just how do we know which diet will work for ourselves without having to go through many fruitless and frustrating ways of eating? This is an important question because every seasoned dieter knows that it becomes harder and harder to lose weight the more diets you try. Instead, the likelihood of putting on more weight increases with every attempt to deprive ourselves of the food and satisfaction we so deeply need. So, it really would be fantastic to find the one eating plan that works for us as quickly as possible.

This books aims at giving you this special eating plan that is tailor-made for your needs, your body type, your food preferences and most of all that will bring you real happiness and satisfaction in all areas around eating.

Instead of giving you yet another book full of food groups, fat grams and detailed recipes I will offer you something completely different. I would like to explain to you the Tibetan Buddhist teachings that I use to help my clients achieve happiness in every area of their lives and apply these teachings to all the issues around eating, weight loss and body image. I have worked in this way for over 20 years with clients in groups and one-to-one. The results have been very positive because virtually everybody lost weight and what is even more important, people became genuinely happy and relaxed with their personal way of eating and body image even if they still had a lot of weight to lose.

I would like to say right from the start that I will not promote a vegetarian or vegan diet in this book.

Even though I myself have been a vegetarian for many years, in Tibetan Buddhism people have always eaten meat and being a vegetarian is not a prerequisite to being a Buddhist. In this book the emphasis will be on helping every individual reader to eat exactly what *they* would like to eat rather than giving them yet another set of overly rigid rules that will be too hard to stick to.

The Buddhist perspective on diet and weight loss

In my work as a Buddhist therapist and teacher I have helped numerous clients to become happier in every area of their life with great success. I have found that Buddhist principles are also invaluable in helping my clients to lose weight and develop a more satisfying and healthier way of eating. These Buddhist principles are:

Relaxation (around the topic of diet and eating, instead of *trying hard* to stick to a diet)

Trust (in your body's in-built drive to stay healthy and slim)

Mindfulness (in every aspect of your food intake and in measuring your weight and size)

Real enjoyment (while you are buying, preparing and eating your food)

Honouring the body-mind connection (when choosing your food and eating)

Love and compassion (for ourselves around all

topics of food intake and body image)

The power of visualisation (through focusing and imagining our desired weight loss goal)

Walking the middle path (between impulsive eating and keeping to dietary rules)

Relaxation

In Buddhist meditation we learn to relax our body and mind and access a state of deep tranquillity. This form of mental and physical relaxation is vital to recharge ourselves, gain insights about our mind and subsequently be more successful in everything we do. In the happy eating approach we use the same principle to relax deeply about all topics around body image, food choices and eating. Instead of *trying hard* to stick to a diet we are simply *relaxing* into the happy eating approach. Tackling the topic of weight loss from this relaxed angle will make it far more likely that we succeed.

If we want to lose weight and stay slim we need to accept one important truth – it is impossible to wear the tight corset of a rigid diet for the rest of our life. It just takes too much effort to suppress our cravings, deprive our needs and ignore our desires. For the average human being with the average amount of willpower, it is impossible to maintain any strict self-depriving diet discipline for any length of time. It simply can't be done because we will run out of energy sooner or later. Some people run out of energy after a month while others run out after a year. But *all* diets are bound to fail if it takes effort and self-sacrifice to stick to them.

The only way to lose weight permanently is by following a way of eating that makes us more and more satisfied and relaxed. This is the promise of the happy eating approach described in this book.

Trust

One of the most basic principles of Buddhism is trust in the inner goodness that is deep within all of us, even if we have many (more superficial) faults. When we transfer this principle to the area of weight loss we can learn to develop trust that our body has an in-built drive to stay slim and healthy and that it will therefore always give out the right signals to achieve this aim.

The happy eating approach will show you how you can let *your own body* be the ultimate diet guru and let it make all the decisions about when, what and how much to eat. You will therefore need very little willpower to follow and remain on your own tailor-made eating plan and even more importantly, eating in this way will feel extremely pleasurable and good. That is why it is called the happy eating approach!

Now I can almost hear the collective outcry from my readers saying that they will never be able to trust their bodies because it was exactly its misleading signals and desires that made them fat in the first place. Not so! The happy eating approach allows you to eat exactly the kinds and amounts of food that will make you feel most satisfied, slim and healthy by listening to the *genuine* needs of your body. Simply put, you will learn how to eat in a way that makes you feel totally good. And I really mean that. I will not try to entice you with a low-fat tofu burger on a cress bed with the false promise that it will give you pleasure even though you don't like it. The way of eating that I will explain to you will show you the art of deeply enjoying every aspect of eating - from going shopping and choosing the tastiest food, to preparing it with love and eating it with great relish. You will only eat tasty food in the amount that makes you feel completely and deeply satisfied. Throughout this book I will show you in numerous ways that you really *can* trust your body to find its own way to its perfect weight.

Mindfulness

One of the most important attitudes that Buddhist students learn is to be very aware of what is going on in their own mind. This mindfulness is indispensible to root out the reasons that have led to our suffering. Learning to be more mindful is also indispensible in the happy eating approach too in order to eliminate the reasons that led to overeating and a negative body image.

In the happy eating approach you will learn to listen to your body and recognise how to feel good about *what* you want to eat, how to feel good *before* you start to eat, how to feel good *during* eating and how to feel good *after* you have eaten. By following these signals very carefully you will make your body into your ultimate diet guru. This means that for a while you will have to forget most of what you have learnt about diets and nutrition so far and eat exactly in the way your body tells you. For many people who have tried and failed at diets, the thought of listening to their own body may feel scary but I can reassure you that this approach may positively surprise you.

You will also learn to become much more mindful around measuring your weight and size (be it with a scale or by using some other device) because many people become overweight simply through avoiding being mindful about their size and weight.

Finally, I will show you how to become aware of any possible deep-seated psychological need to stay overweight. Strange as this may sound, it is a widespread dynamic that is often at play when people find it 'impossible' to lose weight. There is an unconscious part of them that feels that being overweight actually has a hidden advantage, which they do not want to lose. Once this unconscious dynamic has been brought into the light of awareness it will lose its power and you can finally allow yourself to gain the figure of your dreams.

Enjoyment

In Tibetan Buddhism there is a lot of emphasis on learning to *genuinely* enjoy yourself and allow yourself to feel pleasure. In fact, it is said that learning to feel this pleasure is the fastest way to reach enlightenment. Obviously, this is not a book about enlightenment but I found that the principle of actual and genuine enjoyment is beneficial in others areas of our life, as well. It is the very inability to feel pleasure that creates so many problems for people in the Western world. Even though it sounds counter-intuitive, I have found in myself, as well as in the members of my happy eating groups that genuine enjoyment of food is a key factor that helps us to lose weight. Why is this so?

Strange as this may seem, it is the very lack of enjoyment that makes people overeat because they are trying to get this illusive enjoyment through eating more and more while actually feeling increasingly guilty and bloated. Therefore, in the happy eating approach you will find very few diet guidelines other than encouraging you to enjoy your food more fully - and it is this very pleasure that will stop you from making poor food choices and overeating. Once you learn to be fully mindful in this process, it will become easier and easier to actually enjoy yourself while you eat and therefore you will need to eat less and find it easier to make healthier food choices.

In comparison to the joys of the happy eating approach, eating in a way that makes you fat feels like suffering. Many overweight people eat with guilt, feel bloated afterwards and loathe themselves and their appearance. All this will be a thing of the past once you embark on the happy eating approach literally from day one. Instead, you will be eating with relish, feeling satisfied and energetic afterwards, your health and weight will improve and your self-loathing will turn into self-love.

Feeling enjoyment while eating does not mean eating junk food because we cannot *actually* feel pleasure while putting something in our mouth that we know will make us sick. The 'pleasure' of eating junk food is only possible if we do not pay attention and eat in a mindless way. However, the good news is that we do not have to give up the consistency and taste of junk food that makes it so irresistible. We do this through learning how to replace our favourite junk food with equally tasty wholesome foods. The good news is that from the very beginning you will have *exactly* as many sweet foods, fats and carbohydrates as you desire – just the healthy variants of these foods, instead of their toxic counterparts. Interestingly, doing this will add even more to your enjoyment because it will give you an additional pleasure when you know that what you are eating is not only really delicious but also really good for you.

On many popular diets you have to go through an induction phase where you starve yourself and you are promised that you can eat your favourite food again once you have mastered this stage. Unfortunately, many people never make it past the induction phase because it never produces the promised weight loss and they find themselves stuck on a terrible starvation regime. By comparison, in the happy eating approach you will only make changes in your diet when you feel confident that you can stick to them *effortlessly* until the end of your life.

Honouring the body-mind connection

In Buddhism we are taught that all our emotions have an effect on our physical wellbeing and health and that the state of our physical body has an effect on our mind. This body-mind connection is now widely accepted by most people in the Western world but when it comes to diet it seems that most diet gurus have never heard of it.

Virtually all existing diets tell us *what* to eat, *which* amounts to eat and often *when* to eat, too. This is all very well and most people would lose weight on these regimes if only they were able to stick to the guidelines. Unfortunately, they can't because there is one factor that almost all of these diets ignore – people have *feelings* and a healthy diet needs to cater to our emotions as much as it caters to our physical body.

Simply put, we can't treat our body like we treat our car. When it comes to the car it is easy to decide to put petrol or diesel into it, to top up the oil and liquid for the windscreen wipers regularly and then stick to these 'healthy' decisions. It is a different ball game altogether when it comes to the 'engine' that is our body. We might *think* that sweet or fatty food is superfluous but our emotions may strongly demand the sweet or fatty taste in order to feel satisfied. And as I have explained before, anyone who thinks they can override these needs for the rest of their life is simply fooling themselves.

Everyone has strong emotional needs for certain types of foods and tastes and there are many healthy ways of bringing these different foods into your diet. And, as I mentioned before, I am not talking about artificial sweeteners or low-fat cheese. In the happy eating approach outlined in this book you will eat nothing but real and satisfying food.

We are beings with a psyche as well as a body and both these parts of ourselves are completely interwoven. We are psycho-physical beings and nowhere in life can we afford to ignore one part of ourselves at the expense of the other. For example, when we look for a new job we normally ask ourselves whether we can do a particular kind of work physically *as well as* whether it will bring satisfaction emotionally. Whether we plan for a baby, want to build a house or simply plan to go for a holiday, we always ask ourselves exactly the same questions. So why do we think that when it comes to our diet we can override our emotions and rigidly subdue our body? Probably, because nobody has told us yet that this is unsustainable.

In order to lose weight permanently we need to cater to our emotional needs around food as much as we cater to the needs of our body. This is why the way of eating outlined in this book will make you feel emotionally satisfied and physically slim and healthy – all at the same time.

Love and compassion

Buddhist teachings tell us that we can only make positive changes in our life if we can be compassionate with how we are right now with all our flaws and weaknesses. Therefore, the happy eating approach is based on love and compassion for ourselves.

It is exactly this compassion for ourselves that will enable us to return to the happy eating approach once we have fallen off the wagon. And virtually everybody will falter at the beginning of any new approach to food and eating because this is only natural. Learning to eat in a better way can very much be compared to learning a new skill like playing an instrument. It is totally normal to make mistakes in the beginning and it takes a compassionate and kind teacher to encourage the student to keep playing. While adopting the happy eating approach, we need to give this kind compassion to ourselves and in this way we will become successful even if we lose track of this approach many times.

The power of visualisation

In Tibetan Buddhism visualisation techniques are central because they are used to achieve anything we desire, including enlightenment. Our mind and its ability to imagine is very powerful and without the right inner images it will be hard to achieve anything at all. Simply put, if we cannot imagine reaching our goals then it will be nearly impossible to manifest them. I know that this is true because I have seen this principle at work during the last 25 years of using visualisation techniques myself and teaching them to numerous clients. It can be uncanny to witness how seemingly unachievable dreams can be manifested once we use this amazing power of our mind.

In Tibetan Buddhism these techniques are used solely to achieve enlightenment but we should also use them everywhere else in our life because we do not live in a vacuum. Whether we want to reach lofty spiritual ideals or not, it is very important to take care of our body and try to achieve optimal health and an ideal weight. In this book I will show how this goal can be aided through the Buddhist technique of visualisation.

Walking the middle path

Buddhism is famous for its teaching of the so-called middle path, which means finding a working compromise or harmonisation of two seemingly contradictory extremes, e.g. between relaxation and strictness, love and power, striving and letting go. When it comes to diet we need also to find a middle ground between strict dietary rules and impulsive eating. If we are too strict we will fail on any diet and if we are too loose we will not reach our weight loss goal.

The happy eating approach is all about the reconciliation of this seeming contradiction. However, we are not aiming for a lukewarm middle ground where we are a bit strict and a bit relaxed. Doing this would bring about lukewarm results. Walking the middle path in the Buddhist sense of the word means being totally relaxed while totally keeping to the rules at the same time. If this sounds impossible to you, you are not alone. I will show you throughout this book how this seeming contradiction can be resolved. You will learn to feel totally relaxed with your eating while finding a comfortable support with the few rules of the happy eating approach.

The happy eating approach mimics how happy, slim people eat naturally

If you put the advice of the happy eating approach into practice you will arrive at a way of eating that your body-mind was designed for naturally. It is as natural as going to sleep when you are tired and waking up refreshed the next morning. This is not just theory but you can collect your own proof of this claim by talking to the naturally slim people you know. But note that it is only those slim people whose way of natural eating has not been distorted by the advice of the diet gurus. You will find that they all stick to the major principles of this book, often without being aware of them.

When you ask naturally slim people *for what reason* they eat, they look at you with astonishment and say 'because I'm hungry, of course'. If you ask them *what* they eat they say, 'Well, I try to eat healthily but basically I eat what I feel like eating'. And if you ask them *when and why* they stop eating they say, 'because I am full, of course'. The happy eating approach will introduce you to this amazing open secret that has made and kept millions of naturally slim people slender for life.

The happy eating approach describes the way of nourishing ourselves that slim people do *naturally* without calling it a diet.

You don't have anything to lose if you give your own inner body wisdom a chance to come more to the foreground instead of jumping from one extreme 'expert-designed' diet to the next. I honestly believe that the happy eating approach is the *only* way of eating that will make people slim and healthy *in the long-term*. This is not because I have invented a very clever system but because the happy eating approach helps you to eat in harmony with your original body design. Moreover, to my knowledge it is the only system that gives you full satisfaction emotionally as well as healing and nourishing your physical body. This is why it is very easy to keep to until the end of your life.

The happy eating approach is not a diet as such but a way of eating that people can adopt for life without any deprivation or other problem. You will lose weight slowly but continuously and at some point you will find yourself at a weight that you find acceptable and your doctor will not call overweight. However, the emotional suffering from being overweight and having issues around food will stop long before that. This happens because the happy eating approach will help you to make peace with your needs for tasty food and your body image rather than living in an internal war-zone of self-loathing and eating with guilt. Marcy's comment is quite typical for many of my clients:

> *I feel in control. This is the solution to my weight problem forever and ever. I eat when I'm hungry and what I want – apart from sugar. I get the sweet taste from agave nectar so I don't miss anything. I still have a lot of weight to lose but all my suffering has gone. Even at this high weight I feel happy.*

Why it is impossible to fail on the happy eating approach

And here comes some more fantastic news: It is actually impossible to fail in this way of eating because it is not some sort of limited diet but a wholly positive approach that noone will want to give up simply because it feels genuinely good. By comparison, it is common knowledge that 95% of people on ordinary diets fail after some time. This sad fact is part of the confusing reality of the diet jungle. But why is this so?

Basically, people fail on their diets because they are dissatisfying and frustrating in one way or another. Some diets only allow foods that taste bland and boring, other diets deprive us of whole food groups and all too often they simply leave us hungry. No matter what diet we follow, we always find the same scenario: in the beginning we are enthusiastic and put in a lot of effort but after a while we bitterly resent the fact that all the slim people around us are eating with gusto exactly the kind of food we crave but can't have anymore. And sooner or later this bitterness and these cravings will win. They always do - or if we look at the statistics, they win in 95% of all cases.

There is one interesting exception to this rule – and that is trying to lose weight with the help of a slimming club. These clubs seem to have a higher success rate compared with dieting where people struggle on their own. The reason for this can easily be explained: The support of others who are in a similar situation gives people more energy and stamina to stick for longer to the regimes that most slimming clubs prescribe. But if the same people were asked to eat the same limited amounts of foods without the support of the group, most of them would probably give up within a very short period of time. So slimming clubs do work to some extent – but *only* as long as people keep visiting them and accept that starvation and group pressure is the price they have to pay to stay slim. I personally have talked to several rather large ladies who confessed to me that they had been running a slimming club for several years but had gained a large amount of weight as soon as they gave up their job.

By comparison, when embarking on the happy eating approach you will learn to relax more around food, you will learn to enjoy everything around food more deeply and you will learn to love yourself more, no matter how overweight you may still be. Through mindfulness you will learn to come back to these positive states of mind if you happen to fall off the wagon. Can you see that it is impossible to 'fail' on this approach? You can't fail because nobody would want to give up something that feels so good.

My own story

When I was thirteen years old I changed almost overnight from a slim child into a plump teenager. It was a bit of a shock but there seemed nothing I could do about it. I was very energetic and engaged in serious exercise like athletics, jogging and gymnastics almost every day. However, I stayed overweight and had to endure quite a bit of taunting at school.

In my late teenage years I went through a patch of excessive self-starvation which made my body thin but my mind utterly miserable. Unsurprisingly, by my early twenties I was fat again.

Then I started to discover the first principles of the way of eating explained in this book. The biggest help in doing this was reading the books of Susie Orbach whose 'anti-diet' was as much an approach to eating as it was a feminist manifesto. I am very grateful for her work. After writing a food diary for one entire year, my body was slim and my mind was relaxed and confident about eating matters.

Eight years later after I had completed my counselling training, I started to work with people who had problems around eating in groups and one-to-one sessions. Over the years my approach to healing has been constantly improving through combining psychotherapeutic techniques with Buddhist wisdom and my clients usually saw (and are still seeing) impressive results with their problems very quickly.

I myself have stayed slim and happy about weight matters even though my tendency to gain weight easily has remained. I come from a family where virtually everyone is more or less overweight and many are seriously obese. I always gain several pounds in weight when I am on holiday for a week or two and do not have access to my preferred foods. But as soon as I come home the extra weight falls off within a week or so without me trying.

There were only two exceptions from this success story and the first exception was my pregnancy at the age of 38. Even though I should have known better I made the mistake of listening to the pregnancy diet gurus who told me that I should eat biscuits to keep my morning sickness under control. After I had lost touch with the principles of the happy eating approach I gained a staggering 4 stones (25kg) – more than double of what is considered to be ideal. I also allowed myself to be pressurised into eating more than I wanted to when I was breast-feeding. But after my little boy was weaned I regained my slim figure with the principles outlined in this book within 6 months and my mind became contented again around all food issues.

The second problem occurred when I hit my early forties and noticed to my annoyance that my tendency to gain weight had become even stronger (as many people find when they arrive at middle age). What then followed was a period of experimenting with different diets, fasting and making my own diet ever more healthful. After several years of experimenting I have become an even firmer believer in the happy eating approach. It has worked for me all my life and has never let me down. Instead, it has given me nothing but the most delicious food in the quantities I find satisfying.

Now, at the age of 54 I am at an age where many women struggle to keep the weight off their waists and stomachs. But with a BMI of 21.36 I am far slimmer than I was as a teenager while enjoying nothing but the most delicious foods in satisfying amounts. Therefore, if I can do it with my genetic tendency to gain weight easily, so can you. Please follow me along five enjoyable steps to achieve the figure of your dreams while eating as much food as you desire.

Enjoyable step one
Eat when you are hungry

The first enjoyable step of the happy eating approach is concerned with *when* to eat. The answer to this is obvious because nature has given us a clear signal when to eat and that is hunger. If you ask your naturally slim friends for what reason they eat, most of them will say, 'because I am hungry'. Most naturally slim people don't have a rigid meal schedule and they certainly don't purposefully starve themselves in order to stay slim. They simply do the obvious and natural thing - they eat when they are hungry and they don't eat when they are feeling full.

When we eat in line with our hunger signals we can eat without the slightest guilt feelings because what we put into our stomach will be used as fuel over the next few hours if we don't overeat. We can totally trust our body in this respect.

A well-functioning body strives in hundreds of ways to maintain a healthy balance in all its systems. For example, when we are too hot it will make us sweat in order to cool down. When we are attacked by germs it will send out its white blood cells to destroy them. And when it needs more fuel it will send out hunger signals to make us eat. Our body is truly miraculous in its ability to restore balance and health in all our internal systems ranging from a healthy pH-value, an intricate hormonal system to the elimination of its waste products. Why should it want to make us fat? It doesn't have the slightest advantage from having to cope with the strain on digestion, joints and inner organs that excess fat brings. In other words, our body strives for a healthy weight in the same way that it strives for health in general and it is usually successful in achieving this if it isn't overwhelmed by too many toxic influences.

Our body doesn't have the slightest interest in making us fat.

There is one interesting exception to this rule and that is when the body fears starvation. In its own wisdom it immediately starts to put on weight as soon as it fears that food is in scant supply. Most people have had the experience, for instance, of rapidly putting on weight once they have lost a certain amount due to sickness. In a similar way, the body will slow down its metabolism when people starve themselves on a low-calorie diet. As a result, weight loss will be slow and once people stop their diet they will put on weight rapidly so that they usually end up heavier than before.

A similar dynamic happens if we starve our body of whole food groups as it is recommended in some extreme low-fat or low-carb diets. If we deprive our body in this way it will immediately put on weight as soon as we stray from our extreme regime. This reaction is usually interpreted as a confirmation that it is really the carbohydrates or the fat that makes us overweight when in truth it is the dynamic of starving ourselves that is the real culprit.

These examples show that our body has its own

wisdom and power that we can't easily override. On the plus side, we can also learn to trust in our body's strength and use it to our advantage by going with it instead of against it.

In order to be in harmony with our body's natural tendency to maintain a healthy weight, we need first of all to stop starving ourselves in any way.

In other words, we need to feed our body and our psyche with delicious and nourishing food *every* time it demands it in the quantities of fat, protein and carbohydrates it desires. When confronted with this advice many people fear that they would put on even more weight. But let me explain: following your body's impulses means eating only when you are *physically* hungry.

In my groups of overweight women I noticed that virtually *no one* ate in harmony with their physical hunger and that many of them didn't even know how to recognise it. So, at this stage you can ask yourself whether you know what physical hunger feels like and, if so, when you last felt it. If you are like most overweight people, you will find it hard to distinguish between real physical hunger and cravings. In the next few sections we will explore the difference.

Physical hunger versus cravings for food

In order to eat in harmony with our body's wisdom we need to learn, recognise and follow our *physical* hunger signals and distinguish them from food cravings. In the beginning this can be a daunting task because physical hunger and cravings can feel very much alike but with practice most people quickly master this challenge. As an aid, I developed the following chart from my work with many different clients - so the likelihood is great that it applies to you, as well.

Physical hunger	Cravings for food
Physical hunger is triggered by nothing else than the body's need for more energy.	Cravings can be triggered by a wide variety of emotional needs. Some people interpret all negative emotions as hunger and respond to them with eating.
The experience of physical hunger is felt around the physical stomach just beneath the rib cage.	The experience of cravings for food is mostly felt around the mouth and throat.
Physical hunger creates a feeling of a distinct emptiness in the physical stomach.	Cravings for food often go together with emotional feelings of emptiness like boredom, loneliness and feelings of loss.

Physical hunger can feel like a slight cramp in the region of the physical stomach, often accompanied by rumbling.	The experience of emotional cravings can feel like a sucking experience in the mouth with enhanced saliva production.
The cramp of physical hunger can be slightly physically uncomfortable for some people.	Cravings for food can be emotionally painful in a similar way to emotional hurt or jealousy.
Physical hunger can occur with or without the desire to eat. Sometimes we can be physically hungry but may not feel like eating.	Cravings always go together with the desire to eat. People often experience food fantasies.
Physical hunger can happen at any time at any place irrespective of whether food is present. However, strenuous bodily exercise usually shuts physical hunger down.	Cravings for food are often aggravated by seeing and smelling food and particularly by being offered food.
Physical hunger can give us a feeling of bodily weakness. We feel we cannot cope physically if we don't eat.	Cravings for food can give us a feeling of emotional weakness. We feel that we cannot cope emotionally if we don't eat.
Physical hunger disappears when we eat.	Cravings for food often become *worse* when we eat.

For most members of my groups these two columns are like a major revelation and there are usually a lot of 'ahs' and 'ohs' when we explore them. Many people who come to my groups interpret some, if not all, of their negative emotions like sadness, anger and anxiety as hunger signals and respond to them by eating. This dynamic is one of the main reasons why ordinary diet advice fails irrespective of whether it touts a low-carb, low-calorie or low-fat approach. If people eat every time they feel worried or sad, they will gain weight even if they eat zero grams of fat.

I myself experienced this dynamic in a quite a pronounced way when I was pregnant. Every time I felt the slightest feelings of emptiness in my stomach I was possessed by the fear that my baby was starving. Under the sway of this powerful emotion I could not resist the urge to eat and I comforted myself with the thought that I would eat 'normally' again once the baby was born. Unfortunately, I gained much too much weight in this process but I also learnt what it is like to eat for emotional reasons and how strong and irresistible this urge can be.

In my weight loss groups I did *not* find the evidence that people are overweight because of a metabolic disorder called insulin resistance, as many low-carb diet gurus maintain. I found that all the group members – without exception – responded to my two columns by admitting that they ate for many more reasons than physical hunger. In other words, they gave into their cravings on a daily basis and it was this excessive emotional eating in combination with too much junk food that caused their excessive weight.

Giving in to cravings doesn't make people into pathetic beings without willpower. Many members of my happy eating approach groups have a lot of willpower and are successful in many areas of their lives. They simply hadn't heard about the happy eating approach. In actual fact, many of them *overexerted* their willpower by trying to starve themselves, which then automatically created a backlash of binge eating. One of my clients, for example, had been told by her certified nutritionist that she should eat nothing but fish and vegetables three times a day for the rest of her life. My client stuck to this advice for an amazing six months. Now, that is what I call willpower! I myself wouldn't have lasted on this regime for three days. Obviously, at some point my client collapsed under the strain of this overly rigid diet advice and returned to her previous eating pattern of cake and biscuits. Sadly, all she had gained from her nutritionist's advice was a more deeply ingrained eating disorder along with despair.

I don't think I was pathetic either when I was fat as a teenager or during my pregnancy. As a teenager I simply hadn't learnt that I couldn't continue eating as I had done as a child - snacking as and when an impulse arose, often because of physical hunger but many times for emotional reasons, too. Given my genetic background I simply could not afford to continue eating for emotional reasons if I wanted to stay slim. For most people this lesson only comes later at the onset of adulthood or even later when they approach middle age. But the fact remains that eating for any other reason than physical hunger will make people fat sooner or later.

The many advantages of eating in line with our physical hunger

In the following paragraphs we will explore the many advantages of eating in line with our physical hunger.

Eating when we are hungry makes food taste a lot better

You are probably one of those people – just like me – who loves eating. Being and staying slim when you don't care about food is easy; anyone can do that. The challenge starts when food means a lot to you and you want it to be a very satisfying experience. One of the easiest ways of making food taste even more delicious is to wait until you have developed a proper physical hunger. Picture this: you have lost your way in the middle of the mountains and you have run out of food. Slowly you become really hungry, your stomach rumbles and your knees become a little bit weak. Just as you start to get worried you see a little mountain hut that serves simple food to walkers. Once you arrive you discover that you can have nothing but freshly baked crusty bread and butter. How much do you think you will enjoy this food? Probably, this simple meal will taste like it has come straight from heaven! The trick of transforming even the simplest meals into culinary delights is to eat once we are physically hungry.

Eating in line with our physical hunger prevents overeating

'If I wait until I am hungry I will surely overeat', is a common objection to my advice. The truth is that you are much more likely to overeat if you *don't* wait until you are physically hungry. Why is this so? As I have outlined before, many people approach diet and eating as if their body is a machine without feelings. So they think they will eat less if they are not hungry. Unfortunately, this is only true in theory. In reality, our food will be a lot less satisfying if we are not hungry and as a result we will tend to eat *more* in search of this elusive satisfaction! A simple sandwich with butter would never be fulfilling enough if we are not hungry. Instead, we would want a more elaborate meal of some sort or even better – some junk food. But even that cannot really fulfil us if we have not been physically hungry to begin with. So we go on craving even more junk food in order to satisfy what can't be satisfied. In the end we will feel bloated and terribly guilty. 'Why on earth did I eat all this?' we will berate ourselves and the answer is simple – we ate too much because we started eating even though we were not hungry.

Many diet gurus advise us to eat four to six small meals instead of a few big ones – they call it grazing. Again, maybe this would be a good idea if our body was a machine without feelings. But if we try to graze instead of completely satisfying our hunger we will constantly stay unfulfilled. And what will happen as a result? We will eat more! Moreover, who has the time and energy to prepare six delicious meals each day? I haven't. On a six meal diet prescription most people would probably end up reaching for the next best junk food. The outcome of this approach is as predictable as it is sad – if we don't eat deeply satisfying meals we will tend to eat more – and gain weight.

'But doesn't this grazing approach work for some people?', you might ask. As an answer I want to remind you of the overweight ladies I know who used to run slimming clubs. They were slim and the envy of all the participants of the club when they ran it. Their approach seemed to work but the real question is – at what price? Many, many diets bring results for many people – for a limited period of time. At the end of that time the self-deprivation simply becomes too much and people experience a backlash and start bingeing on all their 'forbidden' foods. As a result they become fatter than they ever were. By comparison, the happy eating approach promises to bring results that you can easily maintain until the end of your life without ever having to make real sacrifices.

Eating in line with our physical hunger decreases obsessive thinking about food.

One symptom of having problems with eating is obsessive thinking about food. 'When can I eat? How many calories can I have? Which food is allowed and which one is forbidden? Have I eaten too much?' are typical compulsive thoughts that go through the mind of many overweight people all day long.

The happy eating approach will answer all these questions one by one by teaching you to listen to your body rather than trying to implement some difficult and confusing diet advice. Enjoyable step one of the happy eating approach 'Eat when you are hungry' gives the ultimate answer to the question, '*When* can I eat?' There is no need to think and obsess anymore about this question because it feels intuitively right to eat once your body gives you a clear signal of physical hunger.

Many of my clients have commented on the liberation they felt through this one simple guideline. They reported that the compulsive thinking about diet was drastically reduced or even completely eliminated.

Eating in line with physical hunger eliminates guilt and fear about eating

It is a sad truth that many overweight people feel guilty and anxious about every morsel of food that enters their mouths. Eating in line with our physical hunger will decrease or completely eliminate these guilt-feelings and fears. There is no need to worry anymore that you will gain weight because the food you eat when you are hungry will be burnt as fuel. The people in my groups unanimously say that the happy eating approach relaxes them deeply, takes away guilt-feelings and allows them to enjoy really delicious food.

All anxieties that you will have about starving yourself to become slim will also go away. Starvation is a very painful and often traumatic experience. Many older people who lived through the Second World War had the traumatic experience of starvation and many of them continue to be disturbed by this experience today. It is not uncommon, for example, for people of that generation to stock several big cupboards full of food just to make sure that there is always enough to eat in the house.

Research has shown that virtually everyone who starves themselves on extreme diets develops similar fears and obsessions. Therefore, any depriving diet can bring up deep-seated anxiety, which in turn will lead to overeating. On the happy eating approach you will *always* have enough satisfying food to eat so that you can relax and let go of the fear that you will have to starve yourself in order to become slim.

Eating in line with physical hunger tells the body that it is safe to let go of excess fat

In the same way that our mind can let go of the fear of starvation, our physical body will get the message that it is safe to let go of excess fat. As we discussed before, our body always reacts by storing extra fat if it appears that there is not enough food around. It is one of its many miraculous abilities to cope with the ups and downs of food supply that human beings had to endure throughout history. On the other hand, once the body experiences that there is a constant supply of food it will allow its excess fat to melt away.

A starvation diet is not defined by the number of calories that you are allowed to eat. It is purely defined by how often and for how long you ignore your physical hunger signals. People have incredibly different needs in terms of calories. For example, very muscular people can easily consume 3,000 to 4,000 calories a day and still feel starved. Other people are perfectly satisfied with 1,800 calories. Here we can see again that it is much more important to follow the needs of our unique body. We can then be reassured that we will be satisfied with the happy eating approach irrespective of whether we have a high or low metabolism. Our body will simply show us through its hunger signals how much we need to eat.

Dealing with cravings for food

Many people find my suggestion to eat only when they are physically hungry very reasonable and are prepared to put it into practice immediately. Unfortunately, in many cases they will also experience strong cravings for food that will make it a challenge to eat only when they are physically hungry. On the happy eating approach you will learn to eliminate those cravings step by step until you are completely in control.

Reasons for food cravings

There are a number of triggers that cause craving for food and they can be divided into two main groups: outer reasons for cravings and inner, more psychological reasons. Let's look at the outer reasons first.

Sugar, white flour and deep-fried food: There have been a growing number of scientific studies suggesting that people can become addicted to food in a similar way that people are addicted to drugs and alcohol. One of these studies is called 'Evidence for sugar addiction' and was published by Hoebel, Rada and Avena in 2008. This and similar studies demonstrate that when we cut out junk food, particularly sugar, we can expect real withdrawal symptoms, just like those resulting from drug or alcohol addiction. The most addictive foods by far are sugar, white flour and deep-fried food. Just like drugs, these foods produce a short-term high in our mind and body only to leave us even more dissatisfied shortly afterwards. Therefore, if you have been on a diet high in sugar and white flour you must expect quite a few cravings for a few days. The good news is that these cravings resulting from addictive food will only last for a few days or weeks and will quickly subside.

In enjoyable step two I will go into more detail about how to minimise withdrawal symptoms when you wean yourself off junk food and I can reassure you now that I will also show you a number of ways to find or make equally yummy sweet and fatty foods that you can use to replace your favourite junk food. This will even include things like chocolate.

Starvation diets: The second biggest reason for cravings is the self-deprivation caused by starvation diets. Let me use an analogy to explain how depriving yourself leads to cravings. Imagine you have put yourself on a 'sleep-diet' and tried to get by on six hours of sleep even though you really need eight. As a result you would obviously crave sleep all the time. But instead of giving yourself what you need, you would beat yourself up for being 'weak'. After many months of sleep deprivation you would constantly fall asleep at work and get sacked. Does that sound absurd? Obviously, it is absurd but it is exactly what many people do when it comes to trying to lose weight. They are constantly depriving themselves; then they cave in under their self-inflicted pressure and binge on forbidden food and finally become very fat.

Typically, people deprive themselves most strongly

in the morning and may start the day with fruit and yoghurt in order to be 'good'. Unsurprisingly, they start to feel very hungry from mid-morning onwards but their willpower is still strong so they push themselves through this phase. Lunch then consists of a sandwich, followed by a bar of chocolate as a reward for the starvation throughout the morning because the backlash for their deprivation is already starting. This is then followed by more cravings in the afternoon, which are caused by the sugar in the chocolate and may be managed by drinking lots of coffee or having even more sweets and biscuits. By evening most people's willpower becomes more and more exhausted and results in a big binge that may go on for hours. By the next morning people still feel full from last night's binge and the cycle starts all over again.

As we can see, it is the self-deprivation in combination with eating addictive food that keeps this vicious cycle in motion and throughout this book I will show you how to break free from both these dynamics. You will learn to actually enjoy food while your body becomes slimmer.

Seeing food: Another source of cravings is tempting food that sits seductively in front of our nose and eyes. I myself would find it difficult to sit through a long, boring work meeting in front of bowls of chocolate biscuits. I know that if I ate only one single biscuit it would be very hard not to empty the whole bowl. But not to eat anything in the first place would be as hard as the meeting is boring.

Rigid meal times: Ideas that you should only eat at certain times also contribute to cravings because they either cause you to starve and subsequently overeat or they force you to eat when you are not hungry. As I explained before, eating without hunger contributes to cravings because it is a lot less satisfying than eating in line with our hunger signals.

Upset emotions: The main *psychological* reason for food cravings is the fact that food acts as an effective tranquilliser for all sorts of disturbing emotions. Yummy food definitely calms the nerves and also acts as a pick-me-up when life is harsh, lonely or boring. The members of my happy eating groups reported that they mostly tried to cover up feelings like boredom, loneliness, sadness and worry through eating. Obviously, relying too heavily on the calming and uplifting effects of food comes at the price of becoming overweight. Later on I will show you how to keep the positive effects of food on your emotional well-being without the negative side-effect of becoming fat.

Unconscious psychological dynamics: I have already mentioned that some people have an unconscious dynamic for staying fat. In one of my happy eating groups the following incident happened that demonstrates the point in quite a pronounced way. I was guiding the group through an exercise in which they should imagine that a miracle had happened and that all their excess fat had fallen off over night. I asked the members of the group to imagine meeting all the important people in their life and to look carefully whether they felt somewhat uncomfortable with their new slim figure.

Suddenly I noticed a woman in the group taking a sharp in-breath and becoming fidgety. Later on she told the group that she had remembered a very painful sexual incident and it became crystal clear to her that she had subsequently put on the weight to ward off similar sexual advances. Other clients reported fears of causing pain to a friend or sister by upstaging them and looking better than them. There are many reasons why people may unconsciously hold on to their excess weight and in chapter six we will go into much more detail about this topic. I will show you how to recognise such a dynamic and then how to eliminate it.

How to overcome cravings for food

The happy eating approach works according to the following formula:

The more overall enjoyment and satisfaction we can achieve through eating, the fewer cravings we will experience.

Unfortunately, almost all diets that are available these days totally ignore the emotional aspect of eating. So they simply instruct people to cut out fat or carbohydrates without helping them to cope with losing the comfort of eating these foods. Fat and carbohydrates are the main ingredients of the calming and uplifting properties of food and cutting them out requires extremely high emotional coping strategies that most people simply don't have – or at least not all the time.

In the happy eating approach you will learn how to eat in order to satisfy your body as well as your mind. Therefore, throughout this book you will be encouraged to study the effect of different foods on your physical *and* emotional well-being in order to maximise your satisfaction. In this way you will experience a lot fewer cravings and lose weight. For the moment I will give you a first short overview of how to minimise cravings:

The Do's and Don'ts for eliminating cravings

Do eat when you are hungry: By far the most important advice for eliminating cravings is to eat when you are hungry. And obviously, we are speaking here of the real hunger that comes from your stomach that we discussed earlier on. Nothing causes more cravings than the fear of starvation and as soon as your body and mind can trust that you will stop starving yourself, the sooner your cravings will lessen. If you are totally reassured that you will get something to eat at the very moment your stomach signals that your body has run low on energy, it will be so much easier to ignore all other forms of temptation that may arise during the day.

Don't eat junk food: Sugar and white flour are addictive foods that will produce an awful lot of cravings. Therefore, it is paramount to replace these 'foods' with equally yummy natural foods. I will say more about how to do this in enjoyable step two. You can already be reassured that all junk food will be replaced with real foods and not with artificial sweeteners or low-fat foods.

Don't deprive yourself: Many long-term dieters will find it hard to shed the old bad habit of trying to deprive themselves of what they really want to eat; so they often try to sneak in things like low-fat yoghurts and crispbread when they first embark on the happy eating approach even if they would much rather eat a full-fat dairy product and proper bread. But the more you deprive yourself, the more cravings you will experience. Therefore, eat a really satisfying meal once you are physically hungry. We will go into much more detail about which foods to choose later on.

Don't keep to a rigid meal-plan: Only eat when you are physically hungry and try to organise your life so that you can do that as often as possible. In beginning this may result in eating at odd times like in the middle of the afternoon. But that should not be any matter of concern because after a few weeks you will find that you start having a certain rhythm and then you can start to organise your day around this rhythm. Many workplaces, for example, have flexible lunch breaks and in families the adults don't always have to eat with the children.

Don't snack: If you allow yourself to snack you will encourage cravings because you allow food to be a coping strategy for life's ups and downs. It is much better to get into a rhythm of eating properly when you are hungry and stopping to eat when you are full. It will be much easier to establish this rhythm if you don't have a grey area of snacking in between.

Do rid your environment of all tempting sights of food: Most people can't resist a lovely display of sweets on the coffee table or a bowl of popcorn in front of the television. The easiest way to solve this problem is to put food into the kitchen cupboard or fridge and to banish junk food from the house altogether. Fruit baskets are not a good idea even though fruit is a healthy food. It's just not a good idea to be constantly tempted if you are trying to eat in line with your physical hunger.

Do respond to cravings with something that brings comfort and cheers you up: I admit this is sometimes easier said than done. However, it is not impossible and it will become easier once you make a strong decision that you don't want to pay the price of being fat anymore. But don't forget, we are not talking about eating only celery sticks and exercising for hours. All that is asked of you is to abstain from food as long as you are not physically hungry while knowing that you will have the most delicious meal as soon as you are hungry. The members of my happy eating groups have told me what the most comforting and uplifting activities are that they can do instead of giving into their cravings:

Having a bath

Buying themselves flowers

Phoning a friend

Having a cuddle

Listening to uplifting music

Having a cup of (sweetened) tea

Learning to relax

Remember, you should do these things only if you are *not* hungry. As soon as you feel genuine hunger coming from your stomach you can abandon these activities and tuck into a really satisfying meal.

The last point 'learning to relax' is the most important because cravings for food are ultimately tensions in our body and in our mind. If we can relax these tensions our cravings will lessen. The next section will introduce you to a psycho-physical tool that will help you to achieve this relaxation and reduce your cravings.

Your trump card in conquering cravings

I will now introduce you to a psycho-physical tool that I have used to help many hundreds of people with all sorts of personal problems, including cravings for food. This method is based on Tibetan Buddhist teachings and has an extremely high success rate. It works by visualising (or sensing) a beautiful light in your heart and letting its light radiate out with love. This light comes from the highest source of love and wisdom in the universe – the way *you* define this source.

> ### *Exercise for overcoming cra*
>
> ***Imagine in*** *your heart (in the chest underneath the breastbone sun radiating light in all dire necessary to visualise this ima knowing it is there is enough. Imagine that this light is the source of highest love and wisdom in the universe, the way you define this source.*
>
> ***Let the*** *white-golden light radiate throughout your body and all around you like a comforting blanket. It is a healing and loving light that brings comfort and courage to your troubling emotions and cravings.*
>
> ***Join in*** *with the love of the light and wish yourself to be happy with all your heart. Send love to yourself including all your problems and weaknesses. There is nothing too bad or too weak in you that cannot be embraced by your love and compassion for yourself.*
>
> ***Say to*** *yourself very kindly, 'I love myself with all my weaknesses and problems. I wish myself to be happy and healed.' Imagine being your own best friend giving yourself an inner hug with love.*
>
> ***Work with*** *your inner light and self-love for two minutes twice a day and every time you experience cravings or any other negative feelings around food and your body.*

Some of my clients have initial doubts that working with these inner images will have enough power to them to lose weight. However, once they try simple method their doubts quickly disappear. Here is what two women said after using this method to dissolve their cravings for food. Note, that these are typical results.

Dorothy, 36 years, 80 pounds overweight:

> *I had trouble visualising the light clearly so I talked myself through this exercise rather than seeing anything. I have to say I feel better than I have for many years. I feel a lot calmer and several people at work have remarked on it. Before, I was full of stress and anxiety and I had some paranoia going that everybody is against me. That has changed and I feel my self-confidence is coming back. I think sending love to myself is a key element in this. As soon as I started to work with the light I instantly lost all cravings for sweets and felt no real need any more to eat so much. Also, my portions have reduced dramatically. I could keep to all the rules of the happy eating approach without any difficulty. Before, I ate every evening from the moment I came home until I went to bed. Now I eat like a normal person; I have lost weight and feel more energetic than before.*

Barbara, 56 years, 10 pounds overweight:

> *I noticed that working with the loving light gave me more control everywhere in my life including my eating habits. For example, I tackled a lot of jobs that I should have done a long time ago and I am now able to be tougher with my son who has a drug habit. I feel altogether more positive. Following the rules of the happy eating approach is not difficult and I don't feel deprived. On the contrary, I feel more satisfied after my meals and less bloated. I eat the same amount as before but I have replaced sugar with agave syrup and the weight is coming off nicely.*

There are three key factors that make this method so effective. Firstly, it reconnects us with a source of love and wisdom that is bigger than ourselves. Accessing a source of greater love and wisdom is profoundly healing because we feel we are not alone in this process and that we are getting help.

The second key factor is that this method enables us to send love to ourselves even while we are still overweight. Many overweight people loathe themselves and their inability to stop eating. Often they think about themselves as weak and pathetic. Unfortunately, it is exactly this self-loathing that holds their negative eating habits in place because when we feel so bad about ourselves we need some comfort and this comfort is usually food. Giving ourselves love and compassion will heal this vicious circle and help us to transform our negative habits. Sending love to ourselves means wishing ourselves to be happy and healed – it does not necessarily mean *liking* our excess fat. Therefore, it is always possible to love ourselves, no matter how often we overeat and no matter how much excess weight we carry.

In order to get the maximum effect from this method you should concentrate on this method for two to five minutes twice a day in an undisturbed place. You should also practice it in daily life and the more you can do this *every* time you experience cravings or any other negative emotions around food and weight issues, the more quickly you will be successful.

You will find that it is often enough to simply remember your inner loving light in order to stop yourself from eating when you are not hungry. Also, use this method whenever you feel any form of negative feeling around food and weight issues instead of following the negative feelings. Instead, put your mind immediately on your inner loving light and start sending yourself love as if you are your own best friend. You may be surprised how quickly your mind becomes more peaceful and your compulsive cravings melt away.

The effects of this method are accumulative, which means that you will become more and more in control the more you practice. I will say a lot more about loving yourself in the last chapter. You can also refer to my book *The Five-Minute Miracle* where this method is explained in even more detail.

Frequently asked questions about enjoyable step one

'You say that the body naturally wants to be slim. But aren't there people who are genetically designed to be fat?'

In all the years I have worked with overweight people I never encountered a *single* obese person who only ate when they were hungry. They all, without exception, ate excessively without being hungry. On the other hand, every person I had the chance to interview who was slim without the help of a slimming diet, ate roughly according to the guidelines of the happy eating approach. Therefore, in my experience genes really play a minor role. They may influence whether people look skinny or athletic once they have slimmed down but I have not seen that they make people fat.

'I have been told that I should always eat breakfast in order to raise my metabolism. When should I eat breakfast on the happy eating approach?'

The happy eating approach works irrespective of your metabolic rate because you will simply be less hungry when your metabolic rate is low and more ravenous when it is high. Therefore, in terms of weight loss and well-being your metabolic rate will not make any difference. Let me give you an example from my own life.

> *Twenty five years ago I spent two months in India and I was sick with a*

tummy upset from day one all the way through to day 60. I lost 12 pounds and with a BMI of 18, I was as skinny as a rake. Obviously, this weight loss was virtually all muscle as I didn't have much excess fat to start with and I did not exercise while I was in India apart from walking around. The amount of muscle we have is a main contributor to our metabolic rate and therefore my metabolism went right down.

I did what I had done all my adult life and ate only when I was hungry and stopped when I was full. Unsurprisingly, in the months after my journey to India I found that my need for food had drastically lessened and that I happily existed on rather small portions spaced many hours apart.

But now, after years of muscle-building exercise I weigh more and because my metabolism has increased, as well, I also eat more. However, for my well-being and appearance it makes little difference. I look a bit more muscular, I never starve and I always eat to my full satisfaction.

Coming back to the question about when to have breakfast: In the happy eating approach you will have breakfast once you are physically hungry. For some people this may be shortly after they have woken up while for other people this will mean eating a brunch at 11 o'clock. You can trust that these times are the right times for you and help regulate what *your* body needs in order to achieve its ideal metabolism and weight. However, if you don't have the opportunity to eat breakfast mid-morning it is better to eat something *before* you leave the house, even if you are not hungry. We should always avoid any starvation.

'I tried your advice and ended up eating only two meals a day. Isn't it bad for you to eat in this way?'

Not at all. When your body senses that it is safe to shed weight it will often react by drastically cutting down on hunger signals. As a result you will eat a lot less and lose weight without starving for a single minute. The same process can often be seen in young toddlers who are shedding their excess baby fat. They often refuse to eat for several days which usually worries their parents a great deal. However, this is a perfectly natural process that is designed to bring the child to a healthier weight once they do not need the protection of the baby fat anymore. In the same way the body of an adult will produce less hunger signals once it doesn't fear starvation.

If you find that your body tells you to continue eating three, four or even five meals a day that is fine, too. The bottom line is that you can trust your body and do what it tells you to do.

'I have a fixed lunch break at work. What should I do if I am not hungry at that time?'

Once you know your body and its hunger rhythms you can learn to eat in a way such that you will be hungry at a certain time. You can learn, for example, to adjust your breakfast intake so that you will be hungry again at twelve o'clock for your lunch break at work.

'What about families? If everybody eats in line with their hunger there will be chaos in the kitchen.'

Generally speaking, the happy eating approach can only be introduced to youngsters who are in their late teenage years. Below that age most children simply don't have the abilities that are necessary to stick to its rules. In most cases they would end up eating lots of junk food whenever they felt an impulse. Therefore, children and young teenagers should be fed according to the guidelines that their carers feel are right.

Many families aim to have a meal together once a day. If you aim for such a pattern you can use the same advice given to the question about fixed lunch breaks. I myself have eaten according to the guidelines of the happy eating approach for over thirty years. My husband who was always slim did this as well without being aware of it. In our family, we usually eat dinner together in the evening. Sometimes we eat at different times but that doesn't stop us communicating. When my son was young, for instance, I always sat with him when he had breakfast before school while I ate my own breakfast later.

Through the feedback of my clients I have found that it is not too difficult to organise family life around the principles of the happy eating approach. It may take a few weeks of experimenting but usually things fall quite naturally into place at some point.

'I often get hungry late at night. This is surely not the right time to eat a full meal.'

Research has shown that late night eating has no negative effect on our weight if our overall intake of calories is not too high. Therefore, if you get hungry shortly before you want to go to bed don't starve yourself but eat just the right amount that will keep you going until you fall asleep. The bottom line is that you should never go hungry, nor should you force yourself to eat at times when you have no appetite.

'I find it hard to determine whether I am physically hungry or just experience cravings.'

It can take a little bit of time and patience to figure out when you are physically hungry and when you are not. Generally speaking, if you are unsure whether you are physically hungry or not, drink something and wait until you are sure.

Cravings for food tend to come and go but physical

hunger becomes stronger and stronger until you can't ignore it any longer. However, it can take four, six or even eight hours after a satisfying meal until you are physically hungry again. Some people find it frightening to go without food for up to eight hours but there is no harm in not eating if you don't feel hungry. On the contrary, it is a good sign that shows that your weight loss process is well underway.

The clearest sign of physical hunger is a rumbling stomach or a cramping, empty feeling in the solar plexus just under the rib cage. If you feel hunger signals from anywhere else in your body other than your solar plexus, you should be suspicious. For example, feelings of hunger located in your throat and mouth are usually cravings rather than physical hunger.

One client of mine used to locate her hunger signals in an area below her navel and insisted that she was 'always hungry'. But when she looked more closely she realised that the feeling in her lower abdomen often came and went while the true hunger from her solar plexus only came two or three times a day and disappeared when she had eaten.

'What about tiredness? Isn't that a sign of physical hunger?'

No, tiredness is not usually a sign of physical hunger. In actual fact, in many people tiredness can be a sign of thirst or – more obviously – a sign that they need more sleep. You can try this out. Next time you get a mid-afternoon dip, quickly drink a big glass of water and see if it lifts your fatigue. If you are tired when you had enough sleep and enough to drink, it can be a sign of unresolved emotional conflicts. I see this in my counselling practice all the time but how to resolve this form of tiredness is a topic for another book.

'Do I have to find a quiet place and close my eyes to work with my inner light?'

Work with the image of your inner light for two to five minutes twice a day in a quiet place with closed eyes. At any other time when you experience cravings or negative feelings around food or your self-image, simply think of your inner light and self-love no matter what else you are doing. You can do this in a playful way - there is no need to concentrate hard.

Don't worry if you cannot visualise this light very clearly or if you do not feel a clear feeling of love – in my experience with hundreds of clients I have found that this practice works simply by attempting to do it. If you lose your focus, simply bring your mind back to the light and love for yourself. It will not weaken the effectiveness of this method if you have to repeat this many times.

Pitfalls on enjoyable step one

'I ended up starving and frustrated on the happy eating approach because I couldn't find any food once I was hungry'.

It is a good idea to have your fridge and cupboards well stocked up when you embark on the happy eating approach. I will say more about what kind of foods to buy in step two. For now, I will just repeat that you should never starve yourself in the happy eating approach. If you find yourself hungry unexpectedly have a small snack until you find some proper food. Remember also that you will fall into a pattern of getting hungry after a little while. You can then plan ahead to have food ready for these times.

'I am always hungry.'

It is impossible to be always hungry. If you feel that way you need to carefully distinguish between the signals of cravings and real physical hunger that can be felt in your solar plexus just below your rib cage. Try to respond to your cravings by visualising your loving light or some other form of comfort and eat only when you are physically hungry.

'I don't like to send love to myself. I feel it's too new-agey and it's also part of the selfish 'me-first' culture.'

Stopping self-loathing and developing a benevolent attitude towards ourselves is *the* most important step if we want to transform our negative habits. There is no way around it and it has nothing to do with selfishness or dodgy New-Age practices. On the contrary, loving ourselves is an important and time-honoured Buddhist practice and the *only* way of becoming able to love others. If we can't wish ourselves well, we cannot truly wish others well, either. Therefore, learning to love ourselves may be the single most important piece of advice in this book.

'I have trouble concentrating on the light in my chest and I can't visualise it either.'

Don't worry, just *think* of the light because that will work just as well. You can also make a simple drawing of the white-golden sun and simply look at it while sending benevolent wishes to yourself. It can also be very beneficial to look at your drawing while you are eating.

What to do if you fail to follow enjoyable step one

The happy eating approach is not an approach that you need to follow 100% from one moment to the next. You can allow yourself to ease into it. Therefore, no matter how often you eat without hunger, you are back in the happy eating approach with your next physical hunger. With time it will get easier and easier.

Try not to get angry with yourself for failing to

implement enjoyable step one but remember your inner loving light and say to yourself that you love yourself with all your problems and weaknesses. The more love you can send to yourself the easier it will be to wait for your next physical hunger. Generally speaking, *all* of my clients who have given this technique a serious try had positive results. On the other hand, the people who tried to lose their weight without this help had a much harder time.

The bottom line of enjoyable step one

Learn to recognise your physical hunger in your solar plexus and eat only when you feel physically hungry.

Stop starving yourself in any way. If it is not possible to eat something once you are hungry - try to plan ahead and eat something *before* you get hungry.

Deal with your cravings by practicing your inner loving light or by doing something that comforts you and cheers you up.

Be kind to yourself and send love to yourself with all your problems and weaknesses.

Affirmations for enjoyable step one

'My body will automatically return to its ideal

weight if I eat in line with my hunger.'

'The food that I eat when I am hungry will be burnt as energy.'

'I love myself with all my problems and weaknesses.'

Enjoyable step two
Eat natural food

Physical hunger is the most important bodily signal we have to follow in order to become and remain slim. As you may already have guessed, there is a little catch.

Being guided by our hunger signals instead of counting calories, fat grams or carbs only works with natural foods.

What are these natural foods? Basically, natural food is fresh and unprocessed food. By comparison, non-natural foods are most foods that have gone through an industrial process of refinement (like making brown rice into white rice or producing hydrogenated oil) or food that contains chemicals like preservatives and colouring. Therefore, all foods that contain sugar, white flour or hydrogenated oil are non-natural foods.

It is exactly these non-natural foods that are the *main* cause of obesity in the Western world because they are full of toxins while leaving the body malnourished and producing misleading signals of hunger. Moreover, there is strong evidence that this junk food is one of the main causes for coronary heart disease, many cancers and diabetes.

The British surgeon M. T. Cleaves describes in his ground-breaking book *The Saccharine Disease*, published in 1974, that in societies where people eat only natural food obesity, heart disease and diabetes are virtually unknown. However, once refined and processed foods were introduced and became widespread all these diseases became common place within a time span of twenty years. His findings were so consistent throughout the world that he postulated 'the rule of twenty years'. This rule applied equally to societies who ate a high-fat diet like the Eskimos as it did to African tribes who ate a diet high in carbohydrate. Once these people switched to highly processed and refined foods like white flour and sugar, all the typical diseases of the West became widespread after exactly twenty years. These findings are supported by many researchers who looked at this topic after Cleaves.

Most of us know that fast-food and sugar isn't good for us even if we have never heard about the rule of twenty years. Still, for many of us it is very hard to give up processed food. But why would anybody want to eat something that is so detrimental to our health and looks? The answer is as simple as it is sad – non-natural food is highly addictive.

It is not difficult to prove this statement. There is probably not a single child on this planet who wouldn't prefer brightly coloured sweets or a chocolate biscuit over a wholemeal sandwich. And it is the same with us adults – who would voluntarily forgo cake, white bread and crisps if they were perfectly good for us? I wouldn't.

Continuing to do something that we know isn't good for us is what is called an addiction. Therefore I will refer to non-natural food from now on as addictive food. In fact, just to make my point, I will call it addictive frankenfood! As I have already pointed out in the last chapter, there are a number of scientific studies that have proven the addictive quality of processed foods like sugar and white flour. The main frankenfoods are sugar, white flour, processed fat and industrial food chemicals.

In the second step of the happy eating approach you will learn to wean yourself off these fattening and unhealthy foods and replace them with natural foods, which taste almost as good. I won't lie to you – addictive food 'tastes' better than natural food, particularly if you are still in the phase of a full-grown addiction. But the good news is that for almost any addictive food there is a healthy replacement that will make you feel better in the short run and healthy and good-looking in the long run. In the happy eating approach you can still have the sweet taste in the form of a variety of natural sweeteners like agave syrup or fruit and you can still eat carbohydrates in form of wholemeal grain products or brown rice. You will not be deprived in any way because you can eat as much (healthy) fat, carbohydrates and protein as feels good to you and as long as you choose natural foods over their addictive counterparts.

The negative effects of junk food

In the following sections we will be looking at the health-damaging effects of junk food on our body and mind and how they will slow or prevent any weight loss. These facts are fairly well known but I would like to include them here nevertheless in order to substantiate my claim that the happy eating approach can only work with natural foods. We will also be looking at the problem of ageing and how this makes it harder to lose weight, particularly if we eat too much junk food.

The negative effects of sugar and white flour on our mind and body

All forms of industrial sugar, syrups and white flour are rapidly absorbed by the body into the bloodstream. The sugar in a chocolate bar, for example, releases 30 calories or more into the bloodstream per minute. By comparison, brown rice releases only 2 calories per minute and thus keeps us fulfilled for much longer. It is exactly this quick absorption of sugar and white flour that produces the addictive effect of these foods. They are literally a quick fix for our body - just like taking drugs are a quick fix for our troubled emotions. The problem with most quick fixes is that there is a price to pay for them and while it won't matter if we pay such a price occasionally, it will have a very destructive effect on our mind and body if we indulge in these quick fixes on a regular basis.

In terms of weight loss, the unnaturally quick absorption of addictive foods like sugar and white flour into the bloodstream leads to premature and 'false' hunger feelings - just like a drug junkie craves for another fix once the effects of the previous drug use have worn off. Ultimately, we end up malnourished and overweight even if we eat exactly according to our hunger signals. Here are the main negative effects of sugar and white flour on our body and mind:

Sugar and white flour trigger the release of too much insulin which in turn produces premature hunger signals and weight gain.

Sugar and white flour contribute to low blood sugar. Symptoms include fatigue, irritability, shaking, sweating, yawning, uncontrollable emotions, headaches, light-headedness and nausea.

Sugar and white flour contribute to depression and anxiety because they literally turn us into addicts even if we don't realise it. Being addicted always decreases our healthy emotional coping strategies.

Sugar and white flour use up vitamins and nutrients like Vitamin C, chromium and biotin in order to be digested and in this way they contribute to people being malnourished and more often sick.

Sugar and white flour raise triglycerides, a blood fat that is seen as a risk factor for heart disease when elevated. In fact, many experts now claim that sugar and white flour contribute more to heart disease than fat does.

Sugar and white flour can trigger a host of other negative symptoms like skin eruption and throat problems.

Sugar and white flour contribute to behavioural problems in children because they produce a form of malnourishment.

Sugar is a main cause of dental cavities.

Sugar is said to break down collagen and increase wrinkles.

Excessive sugar and white flour are the main contributors to the onset of Diabetes 2.

The negative effects of processed fat on our mind and body

Processed fats include all refined oils (most oils that you can find in your local supermarket) along with all processed animal fats such as in powdered milk and eggs, which are found in virtually all processed foods. The worst of all processed fats is hydrogenated fat which is vegetable oil that has been injected with hydrogen at high temperatures to prolong its shelf life. Hydrogenated oil can be found in virtually all processed foods like biscuits, cakes, crisps and margarine, as well as in all deep fried food and is the staple fat in *all* fast-food.

Nutritionist Bruce Fife explains in his book *Eat Fat, Look Thin* that all processed fats are more or less oxidised. Oxidised oil and fats produce large amounts of free radicals and, according to Bruce Fife and many other experts, it is these free radicals that lead to arteriosclerosis and later on to heart disease.

By comparison, natural fats include those that occur in foods like nuts, seeds and avocados, all unrefined, cold-pressed oils (like cold-pressed virgin olive oil) and the saturated fat found in fresh meat and dairy products. According to Bruce Fife and contrary to widespread belief, these natural fats are not detrimental to your heart or health in general. He explains that people all over the world have eaten natural fats, including animal fats, in large amounts for thousands of years without *ever* dying of heart disease. The first deaths from heart attacks were only recorded roughly one hundred years ago – exactly when people started to eat a diet higher in sugar, white flour and refined oils.

However, even though the fresh saturated fats from animal sources don't seem to be the main culprit that has caused heart disease in Western societies to sky-rocket, they are still not entirely good for us because they do contribute to arteriosclerosis, which is the main cause of heart disease. A healthy individual would probably cope easily with the arteriosclerosis caused by saturated fat from fresh produce but most of us cannot necessarily assume that we are that healthy. Particularly if we have had a diet rich in processed foods in the past or we have a family history of heart disease, we should go easy on animal fats.

As I mentioned above, the very worst fats are hydrogenated fats. Professor Walter Willet who researches fatty acids at the Harvard School for Public Health has stated that hydrogenated oils are two to three times as bad as saturated fat in terms what they do to blood fats.

In terms of weight loss, eating healthy fats is actually good for you. Many people will find this statement amazing – even shocking - because we all have been indoctrinated by the 'low-fat brings low weight myth'. I will explain more about the weight loss promoting quality of fats in enjoyable step three. For the moment let's look at the negative effects of processed fats on our mind and body as explained by Bruce Fife and in Ann Gittleman's book *Eat Fat, Lose Weight* where these facts are explored in great detail and supported by many scientific studies:

Processed fats lead to heart disease.

Processed fats are linked to diseases like multiple sclerosis, allergies, arthritis, diabetes and cancer.

Processed fats interfere with the body's ability to process and utilise healthy fats. Once the body is deprived of essential oils it will crave more and more fat and thus make us fat.

Lack of healthful fats contributes to mental disease, anxiety, depression and an abundance of physical ailments and diseases.

Some experts call hydrogenated oils the most deadly poison that we commonly eat.

The negative effects of food additives on our mind and body

Food additives are E numbers, preservatives, food colouring, artificial sweeteners and salt. Strictly speaking, these chemicals are not addictive as such but because they often come in the package of refined carbohydrates and processed fats, I will lump them together with addictive foods. Also, some E numbers are perfectly harmless like Vitamin B2, for example, which is used as a food colouring. Unfortunately, the scope of this book doesn't allow me to go into great detail about which food additive does what to our mind and body. Therefore I will give here only a rough outline.

The list of harmful effects of artificial sweeteners is long and gruesome. Particularly aspartame (found in many processed foods, drinks, vitamins and medicines) has been blamed for a wide variety of health hazards ranging from confusion and abdominal discomfort to severe illnesses. Other artificial sweeteners are also associated with a wide range of negative bodily and mental symptoms.

Artificial sweeteners and glutamates (flavour enhancers) can cause drastic insulin spikes which in turn lead to abdominal discomfort, premature hunger signals and weight gain. The American Cancer Society has found that people who regularly use artificial sweeteners actually have an increased appetite and tend to gain weight.

Many E-numbers, food colouring and preservatives have been blamed for causing intestine upsets, worsening asthma, allergies, behavioural problems and hyperactivity in children as well as mood swings and irritability in adults.

Too much salt causes oedema and weight gain and contributes to high blood pressure and heart disease. (A little salt is healthy and beneficial.)

The negative effect of ageing for weight loss and staying slim

Some people may now object and say that there are plenty of slim people who can eat a lot of fast-food and still stay slim. The answer is that the majority of people in our society lose their slim body once they are past the age of forty. Therefore, the slim people who can afford to eat junk food are probably young or part of a very small group of people whose genes prevent them from ever becoming fat (but not necessarily healthy). The eating habits outlined in this book are copied from people who stay slim *throughout* their lives, even if they don't have a single 'slim gene' (like myself, for example). Generally speaking, slim people don't eat junk food.

Growing older and becoming fat seems almost inevitably linked in our society but it doesn't have to be that way. Men and women from societies all over the world who eat natural food stay slim throughout their lives and, even more importantly, they develop illnesses like cancer, heart disease and diabetes less often. If we follow their example it will be almost guaranteed that we regain a slimmer and healthier body.

Generally speaking, the body finds it much easier to store calories as fat rather than burning them up as energy. Therefore, when we become older and our digestive organs lose their full capacity we don't become thinner and thinner, we become fatter and fatter. This is the reason why people tend to put on extra weight when they age even if they don't change their eating habits or exercise routines. It is the same dynamic that makes even young people fat if they eat a lot of toxin-laden junk food. The more toxins our body has to deal with, the less capacity it has to burn food as energy and instead will take the easier route of storing calories as fat.

Weight loss occurs only under two conditions: The first is an efficient healthy organism that is not overloaded with calories or toxins. In this case the body will naturally strive to achieve a healthy weight just in the same way as it strives to be healthy in all its other systems. The second condition of weight loss is extreme stress like starvation or a disease like cancer which will cause the body to literally waste away. If we are somewhere in the middle and give our body stress by wolfing down toxin-laden junk food, even a low-calorie diet will make it hard to lose weight.

What exactly can I eat in the happy eating approach?

Basically, in the happy eating approach you can choose *any* natural food you want and the more you eat *exactly* what you feel like eating, the more successful you will be. The 'art' of making these choices will be explained in more detail in enjoyable step three. For the moment I will give you a list of the natural foods that can be enjoyed until you feel fully satisfied and a list of the addictive foods that will interfere with weight loss and good health if consumed in too great a quantity.

You may ask how strict do you have to be to always choose natural foods in the happy eating approach? Well, there is certainly plenty of leeway and I do not claim that the following two columns are the be-all-and-end-all regarding food choices. There is constant new research in nutrition, which tells us of hidden benefits or dangers of certain foods that we have not been aware of before. For that reason, please do not regard the following list as some sort of bible but only as a general guideline about making reasonably healthy food choices and feel free to add or delete foods according to your own ideas about what is healthy or not.

You will certainly not drop dead or expand four inches each time you eat a biscuit or a packet of potato crisps. But as I have already pointed out, it will get harder to stay slim as we get older because the bad habits of our youth will accumulate and many people find that they just don't get away anymore with eating addictive food even in small quantities. I myself are one of these people and I have found that even small amounts of sugar makes me put on weight very quickly. But I don't really mind that as I get plenty of sweetness from the healthy sweeteners that I will describe further down. All I can say is that if you keep to the natural food column you will feel better in your body and in your mind. The choice is yours.

Natural foods	*Addictive frankenfoods*
Grain products All whole grains like brown rice, whole wheat, quinoa, buckwheat, millet, spelt and whole oats, etc; all pasta and bread made from wholemeal grains; all flakes for muesli and all breakfast cereals made from whole grains and without added sugar; cake and biscuits made with wholemeal flour, high quality fat and natural sweeteners	White rice, bread and pasta made with white flour; 'brown bread' as this is made with white flour, too; all breakfast cereals which are not wholemeal or which have added sugar; all cakes, biscuits or other foods made with white flour, processed fat and sugar.
Vegetables, pulses, fruits, nuts and seeds All freshly cooked and raw vegetables, salads and fruits, fermented vegetables like sauerkraut, cooked or baked potatoes; all nuts and seeds; all fresh and dried pulses like beans, lentils and soy products	Commercially produced chips, crisps and other potato and vegetable products
Dairy All cheese without preservatives or colouring; yogurt (sweetened with natural sweeteners), butter, milk, all other dairy produce without sugar, preservatives or colouring (natural sweeteners are fine)	Powdered milk found in many processed foods; all dairy produce with sugar, preservatives or colouring
Meat, fish and eggs All fresh and if possible organic meats; all fresh fish	Processed meat like sausage and cured meat;

from uncontaminated sources (much of farmed and ocean fish is contaminated; organically farmed fish seems to be a safer bet); fresh eggs (preferably organic and free-range)	processed fish; powdered egg found in many processed foods
Fats Butter, cream and animal fat (in moderation); virgin cold-pressed oils made from vegetables and nuts (like virgin olive oil or coconut oil); fats that are naturally occurring in fresh food like avocados, fish and nuts	All refined oils (typically, all oils in a regular supermarket are refined apart from virgin olive oil); hydrogenated oil that can be found in almost all processed food
Sweeteners (in small quantities) Agave syrup (a sweetener made from the agave cactus that doesn't raise blood sugar); stevia (a non-caloric herbal sweetener), xylitol (a natural sweetener made from birch bark)	All forms of ordinary sugar, artificial sweeteners, glucose, syrups and treacle; all sweets and all foods containing ordinary sugar
Beverages Water; herbal teas, green tea, red wine in moderation	All drinks that contain sugar, sweeteners, colouring and other chemicals
Miscellaneous Vinegar, fresh and dried herbs	All food that contains sugar, unhealthy fat and other food additives

These two columns will give you a rough idea of what you can eat to become and stay slim in a healthy way but you probably have already noticed that it will be nearly impossible to stick one hundred percent to the natural food column. For example, even the best organic wholemeal bread usually contains a small amount of refined oil. You could also argue that xylitol is a highly processed food and you would be right. These two columns don't cover a grey area of foods, either, that is neither fresh nor a real frankenfood. These foods include lightly processed foods without sugar, preservatives or hydrogenated oil like tomato sauce in a jar or tinned vegetables.

In these cases you need to use your own common sense to decide what is good for you and what is not. As a rule of thumb, you should never eat anything from the addictive frankenfood column more than once a week. The good news is that you don't need to be rigid about your food choices as long as you understand what really harms your body and get the majority of your food choices right.

Healthy preparation of food is an act of love

You probably have guessed by now that take-aways and grabbing some pastries from your nearest bakery is incompatible with the happy eating approach. Even though I admit that these kinds of foods can give you a short-lived sense of 'feeling good' they are no replacement for food lovingly prepared in your own kitchen, which can *really make you happy.*

I have worked with clients who *never* go to the supermarket to buy fresh food and who obtain all their food by going to the nearest take-away. Unfortunately, there is no way to be happy with your body long-term if you eat in this way (let alone losing weight) even if you choose the 'healthiest' take-aways. On the other hand, virtually all the foods listed in the natural food column can be bought in regular supermarkets with a little bit of looking around and careful studying of food labels. The only exception is the sweeteners and I am afraid that there is not a single non-fattening and healthy sweetener to be found in most regular supermarkets. However, you will find them readily on the internet or in a healthfood shop. I will say a few more things about these sweeteners a little bit further down.

If you choose natural foods you can eat anything and everything you like from pizza to cake and from pudding to chips. The happy eating approach doesn't ask you to give up any of your favourite dishes if you prepare them with natural and fresh ingredients and eat them when you are hungry. For example, you can make a great pizza by using a wholemeal pizza base from your healthfood shop (or making it yourself) and replacing the salami with some organic minced beef. You can make healthy chips by cutting up fresh potatoes, drizzling them with coconut oil (which does not oxidise at high temperatures) and baking them on a tray in the oven. You can also enjoy cake and pudding by preparing them with the ingredients from the natural food column.

Unfortunately, there are always people who complain that cooking healthy food every day is too much work. When I discuss possible meals with some clients, some of them look at me aghast and say, 'but that would take some planning!' as if that is totally out of question. If you feel the same way, please honestly answer the following question before your read on: *What is really more important than cooking meals that will make you (and your family) healthy and slim?*

I personally think that feeding my body and those of my family for optimal health and well-being has priority over almost anything else that I do all day long. For me it is equally important as getting enough sleep and obviously also working to make ends meet. But anything else comes second. In other words:

Preparing healthy food is an act of love for ourselves and our family.

Cooking healthy food really is an act of love because it significantly contributes to the well-being of everybody. Moreover, if our children see that working in the kitchen is a worthwhile activity, they will easily follow our example and adopt the same habit when they have grown up. Isn't that a worthwhile message to pass on?

If you want you can emphasise the loving aspect of food preparation even further and make it into a spiritual act. Here is what Dr. Sanjay Parva writes about Ayurvedic cooking in an article in *Positive Health* magazine.

> *Anything that involves love is spirituality....Spirituality does not necessarily require a lifestyle devoted to religious practices such as going to church or temple, making offerings, saying prayers and so on. Cooking offers an ideal everyday and priceless opportunity to be spiritual....You begin the day with a spiritual outlook, which is derived from cooking, and whatever you do for the rest of the day becomes an extension of a spiritual practice you started in the morning. The outlook lingers on till the next dawn and grows and continues day by day.*

If we have to operate on a tight schedule we can take advice from Jane, who is a busy working mother but manages to cook healthy food every day. Jane organises her shopping and only goes to her local supermarket once a week. She cooks daily but she sticks to simple meals like stir-fries and stews in which all the ingredients go into one pot. In addition, she prepares wholemeal pasta or brown rice twice a week in advance and adds these to the family meals as she needs them. Keeping pre-prepared complex carbohydrates (wholemeal pasta or brown rice, for instance) in the fridge doesn't deduct anything from their wholesomeness and makes creating healthy meals a lot faster.

If you are out and about you don't need to rely on

the nearest take-away to feed yourself and your family, either. With a little bit of planning ahead you can prepare yummy wholemeal sandwiches with sweet or savoury toppings to meet every taste. It is satisfying and a lot cheaper than eating out, too. If you don't mind spending the money, you will find that most restaurants offer plenty of choices that fit into the natural food column. One of my clients, for example, often orders meat with a double portion of vegetables while forgoing the chips and white pasta.

How to wean yourself off addictive frankenfood

If your eating habits so far have included large amounts of addictive food I recommend that you wean yourself off these foods one by one and bit by bit and not all at once. This patient approach is important because otherwise you may easily fall off the wagon and give up on the happy eating approach. It may take you a few months before you are off all the addictive frankenfoods and that is perfectly okay. In fact, it is almost better than doing it all at once because you can be more assured that you can keep to your new and healthier food choices if you have made the change very slowly. By comparison, any radical attempt to change your food choices all at once will increase the danger of experiencing a massive relapse.

While you are weaning yourself off sugar, white flour and unhealthy fat it is important to stick to enjoyable step one and always and only eat when you are physically hungry. Doing this will usually be enough to kick-start a first wave of weight loss.

Weaning yourself off sugar

The most important (and for most people most difficult) frankenfood is sugar and I suggest that you start just there. Once you are off these sweeteners everything else will be quite easy because sugar is the most addictive food of all. But remember, you are not asked to give up the sweet taste altogether; you just have to make that little bit of extra effort to replace ordinary sugars and syrups with the sweeteners from the natural food column.

Everybody needs some sweetness in their life and the happy eating approach will show you how to get this taste without sacrificing your health and weight loss in the process.

In my experience, the safest options for bringing sweetness into your life without endangering your health and weight loss are agave syrup, stevia and xylitol. I have clients who eat homemade biscuits made with agave syrup or stevia every day and lose their weight nicely. I myself love strong green tea sweetened with xylitol and I drink it all day long. Here is a short overview of the healthy sweeteners and what benefits they have for your body.

Agave syrup: Agave syrup is the raw, unprocessed juice of the agave cactus that is cultivated mostly in Mexico. It contains mostly fructose (fruit sugar) and has been used for centuries by the indigenous people there. No adverse side effects have ever been reported. The best news about agave syrup is that it doesn't raise blood sugar and therefore doesn't produce premature hunger signals like ordinary sugar and syrups do.

The glycemic index measures how much blood sugar will be raised by certain foods and agave syrup is at 10, which is very low compared with 100 for ordinary sugar. Agave syrup tastes like a very mild honey and doesn't change its taste in hot drinks, which makes it ideal to use in tea and coffee. In the German speaking world, agave syrup is the staple sweetener of most health conscious people.

Stevia: Stevia is a non-caloric herb that has been used as a sweetener for centuries by indigenous people in South America. It is many times sweeter than ordinary sugar and doesn't raise blood sugar at all. Not everyone likes the taste of Stevia (it tastes rather like an artificial sweetener) but, on the plus-side, Stevia actually has the health benefit of lowering blood pressure. There have been no reports of adverse side-effects from the use of Stevia.

Xylitol: Xylitol is a sweetener that is made mostly from birch bark and it looks and tastes exactly like ordinary sugar. The glycemic index of xylitol is very low at 7. This sweetener has been extensively researched for many decades and no adverse side-effects have been found. On the contrary, xylitol has plenty of health benefits – it delays and even reverses tooth decay and helps prevent osteoporosis, ear infections and sinusitis.

You may wonder why I don't recommend other natural sweeteners like honey, molasses, malt, fruit juices and dried fruits like raisins. Unfortunately, not everybody is able to continue losing weight while using these sweeteners even though they are natural and contain many healthy nutrients. The reason for not including these sweeteners is that they can raise blood sugar and produce premature hunger signals in susceptible individuals, just as sugar does. This may have to do with a genetic predisposition or it may be caused through a lifetime of over-consumption of sugar.

One of my clients, for example, told me that she had gained a lot of weight during the time she consumed daily freshly squeezed fruit juices instead of breakfast. These juices contained a lot of wonderful nutrients but their high sugar content led to weight gain despite their healthfulness. You will have to try out for yourself if you can continue losing weight if you use natural sweeteners. If you can't, simply stick to agave syrup, stevia or xylitol to sweeten your food and drinks.

Generally speaking, the wise use of sweet foods are the make or break of your weight loss. If you eat too much sugar or sweet foods other than agave syrup, stevia and xylitol you may be sabotaging you weight loss more than with any other 'cheat'. In actual fact, I have observed in several of my clients, as well as in myself, that even a teaspoon full of sugar a day can lead to weight gain. This weight gain doesn't result from the few calories of the teaspoon full of sugar but from the hunger-inducing effects that sugar has on our body chemistry. For this reason it is so important that we refrain from refined sugar and white flour in the happy eating approach and stick to healthy sweeteners and wholemeal carbohydrates. There is no need to cut our carbs as so many diets advocate. Simply replacing them with the healthier options is all we need do. Doing so will not only be good for our weight loss but also for our health in general.

If you have eaten a lot of sugar you may experience some withdrawal symptoms once you try to come off it. It is therefore wise to wean yourself off the sugar slowly. You can simply do that by replacing your daily sugar intake bit by bit with a healthy sweetener of your choice. If you do this slowly enough, it is unlikely that you will experience withdrawal symptoms.

However, for some people this slow process may not suit them and they will want to give up sugar all at once. In that case they may experience some withdrawal symptoms. One client of mine complained that she felt like weaning herself off heroin because she experienced flu-like symptoms and felt very miserable. The withdrawal symptoms may last a few hours or a few days and could include one or several of the following list:

Fatigue

Emotional instability and a feeling that everything gets to you

Unusual anxiety, depression and irritability

Flaring up of physical symptoms

A general feeling of being 'under the weather'

I personally believe that the high success rate of low-carb dieting is largely due to the fact that it gets people off sugar and white flour. It would also explain why so many people feel so miserable in the first two weeks of doing it. Most of my clients have had a stint at some low-carb dieting before they came to see me but they consistently report that they couldn't stick to it even though they lost some weight. By comparison, the happy eating approach allows you from the start to keep (healthy) sweetness and carbohydrates in your diet, which makes this approach so much more doable *long-term*. The sweet taste and carbohydrates in general are a strong emotional need for most of us and if we try to ignore this desire we shouldn't be surprised if we fail on our diet. We will be looking into the emotional need for certain foods in more detail in the next chapter.

Once you are through the sugar withdrawal phase, I recommend that you take a few weeks to become comfortable eating only food with healthy sweeteners. For some people this will be very easy while for others it will require major changes to their diet. Changing our diet is difficult because most people are so very attached to what they eat. This is why I suggest going slowly and making sure you feel fine physically and emotionally with every change in your diet before tackling the next one. All the while, you should stick to enjoyable step one and eat only when you are physically hungry. In the vast majority of cases this will be enough to kick-start your weight loss.

Weaning yourself off refined white flour

The next step is to get *all* white flour and white rice out of your diet. For most people this means switching to wholemeal pasta, wholemeal bread and brown rice. You should also prepare all your cakes and biscuits with wholemeal flour from now on. Compared with getting rid of sugar, this step is rather easy.

The only hard bit is coming to terms with the fact that there are so few (if any) wholemeal products available when you are out and about. Unfortunately, even if you do find wholemeal sandwiches in a chilling cabinet you have to be careful. A glance at the food label often reveals a shocking array of chemicals to keep these products 'fresh'. These sandwiches often languish up to a week on the shelf and only appear fresh because they are loaded with chemicals which will be a burden for your health. The obvious solution is to take some old-fashioned home-made sandwiches with you, which requires a little bit of planning ahead. Again, I recommend that you take a few weeks until you feel really comfortable with only eating wholemeal products before you tackle the next step.

Weaning yourself off unhealthy fats

Weaning yourself off unhealthy fats can be hard for

people who are addicted to deep-fried junk food. It means forgoing foods like crisps, commercially prepared chips, onion rings, fish in batter and all other deep-fried food. The good news is that you can prepare all these foods at home with healthy fats.

The happy eating approach is not a low fat diet.

Fat is another food that we need for our emotional satisfaction. If we eat too little we will often overcompensate by eating too many carbohydrates – particularly sugar. Therefore, preparing our meals with a really satisfying amount of healthy fat is essential. Here is a short overview of healthy fats as recommended by Bruce Fife and many other nutritionists.

Cold-pressed virgin oil from vegetables, seeds or nuts strengthens the immune system, lowers cholesterol, removes water retention, stabilises blood sugar, increases fat-burning, improves digestion, improves hair, nails and skin, strengthens bones and reduces the risk of heart attack. These oils also help to lift one's mood and alleviate depression.

Omega 3 oils found in fish and flaxseed have a particular long list of health benefits. In addition to the general benefits of cold-pressed oils they improve the mood, behaviour and learning abilities in children and adults. They also inhibit tumour growth, improve arthritis and make us look younger by increasing the elasticity of our skin.

Virgin coconut oil is a saturated oil but it doesn't

carry the health risks associated with saturated fat from animal sources, according to nutritionist Bruce Fife. On the contrary, it is said to help with thyroid health, raise metabolism, promote weight loss and it has anti-fungal, anti-viral and anti-bacterial properties. It is also said to reduce the risk of heart disease, cancer and other degenerative diseases. I myself found coconut oil invaluable to cure the Candida infections that I suffered from a great deal when I was younger.

Cold-pressed oils (apart from coconut oil) must be kept in the fridge and shouldn't be used for frying because that would quickly damage them. Instead, you can pour some of these oils over your food *after* you have cooked it. For frying you can use coconut oil because it remains stable even at high temperatures.

Weaning yourself off too much salt

Weaning yourself off too much salt shouldn't be too difficult once you have rid your diet of overly salty junk foods like chips, pretzels and salami. The taste for salty food is acquired and is as equally addictive as all other unhealthy food choices. Luckily, it is not that difficult to reverse this trend. Simply salt your food so that it is *just* salty enough for your taste. As you continue to do that, your salt intake will gradually go down. As a general guideline, nutritionists recommend that we shouldn't eat more than a teaspoon of salt in a day.

Frequently asked questions for enjoyable step two

'Can I drink tea and coffee in the happy eating approach?'

Some people are sensitive to caffeine and it will undermine their efforts to lose weight. Feel free to try out how much coffee and tea you can afford and also remember that coffee is not exactly a healthy drink. If you are a tea drinker you can simply switch to green tea which is not only healthy due to its antioxidant content but is also said to have weight loss promoting properties. If you like coffee try to limit your consumption to one or two cups a day and see what happens.

'What about beer and fruit juice?'

Most people will get away with the occasional glass of beer or fruit juice if it stays occasional. But if you drink too much of these beverages every day, you will probably find it hard to lose weight.

'Can I eat frozen food in the happy eating approach?'

According to Ayurvedic and traditional Chinese medicine, frozen food is deplete of 'chi' (life-force). This means that despite the fact that it contains many vitamins and minerals, it is said to be weakening in the long-term. The same is true for cooking with the microwave.

'I have eaten food from your healthy food columns for years; I exercise every day and I eat less than the people around me. Still, I can't lose weight.'

I've had quite a few clients with this complaint and unfortunately not a single one stuck to step one and only ate when they were hungry. Unfortunately, it is perfectly possible to overeat even the healthiest food – and overeating is the *main* reason for weight gain. Therefore, in terms of weight loss, enjoyable step one – 'Eat only when you are hungry' – is the most important.

Pitfalls for enjoyable step two

'In the happy eating approach you can't eat out because you can't get natural food in restaurants.'

No, you can go to restaurants – you only have to avoid fast-food restaurants. In a proper restaurant you can always order meat, fish, vegetables, potatoes and salads and you needn't worry if there is a little bit of sugar in the gravy or if the meat isn't organic. However, if you want to lose weight you will have to stay away from deep-fried food, refined carbohydrates and sugary desserts. (By comparison, at home you can make yourself as many sweet dishes with healthy sweeteners as you desire.)

'The food from the natural food column is too expensive.'

Eating fast-food and prepared meals is far more expensive than buying fresh food from your nearest supermarket and preparing it at home. I admit that the price of the sweeteners I recommend can be a bit of a shock. Still, I think your health and well-being should be well worth that expense. There are many areas in everybody's life where we can be more frugal but in my opinion diet should not be one of them. For example, it will not harm us in the least to wear cheap clothes or go on a cheap holiday but it will harm us a great deal to eat cheap food. This doesn't mean that we should buy exorbitantly expensive fruit that has travelled halfway round the world – seasonal and locally grown food will do just fine and is usually very reasonably priced.

'I don't have the time to prepare natural food'.

I have quite a few clients who have this problem. Generally speaking, finding time is always a case of priorities. You know the old saying 'where there is a will, there is a way' – one can equally say 'where there is a will, there is time'.

'The happy eating approach doesn't make me feel good because I miss my chocolate.'

You should not eat commercial chocolate but it is perfectly possible to bring the chocolate taste into your diet by using chocolate powder which you can spread and mix into virtually all sweet foods. You can also mix it with ground nuts and agave syrup to make a delicious spread for sandwiches.

What to do if you fail to follow enjoyable step two

First of all, be kind to yourself and send love to yourself with the method that we discussed at the end of enjoyable step one. The more love you can send to yourself with all your problems and weaknesses, the more quickly you will be able to put your positive resolutions into practice.

In terms of weight loss, some people will get away with a lot of cheating on enjoyable step two while other people won't. But cutting out junk food is not only about weight loss. It is quite literally a question of life and death. Therefore, if you cross the fine line where you sabotage your own health and weight loss goals by eating too much addictive foods, it is often beneficial to give them up completely. With our addictive habits, it can sometimes be easier to make a clean cut in the same way as it is easier to stop smoking completely instead of smoking a little bit.

If you catch yourself bingeing on junk food, first of all relax. Nothing awful will happen – you will not gain five pounds in an instant and you will not drop dead, either. Then slow down your eating and try to really relish your food. As you will learn in enjoyable step four, really relishing your food is an enlightening and transforming experience. Once you allow yourself to really enjoy your food you may need a lot less of it compared with wolfing it down in a guilt-ridden and half conscious fit.

The bottom line for enjoyable step two

Wean yourself off addictive frankenfood bit by bit and not all at once.

After a few months you should have eliminated 98% of your food intake from the frankenfood column.

If you do eat junk food, do it consciously and try to enjoy it as much as possible.

Affirmations for enjoyable step two

Natural foods make me naturally slim.

Preparing healthy food is an act of love for myself and others.

Enjoyable step three
Eat only what you really feel like eating

Don't you love the title of this chapter? While enjoyable step two was probably reminiscent of much common sense diet advice, the happy eating approach will now become seriously different from anything that you may have heard before.

Eating what you feel like eating has two aspects: You need to choose food that you really feel like eating *and* that will also make you feel good afterwards. By choosing food that you feel like eating *and* simultaneously envisioning how it will make you feel once you have eaten it, you will become more and more sensitive to your body and mind's needs. In this way you will learn to respond to these needs - eating exactly what will bring short-term *and* long-term satisfaction.

Choosing exactly the food you desire is the great freedom of the happy eating approach. It is this freedom that will make sure that you can stick to it until the end of your life.

If you ask the naturally slim people you know what they eat, most of them will say something along the lines, 'I try to eat healthily but mostly I eat what I feel like eating.' Naturally slim people *don't* deprive themselves like many people do who struggle with a weight problem. One of my clients, for example, stayed on a starvation diet every year for six months and for the other six months she binged on all the food that she didn't allow herself before. In this way her weight swung back and forth without ever reaching a satisfying level. However, once I introduced her to the idea of *always* eating what she felt like eating she finally started to lose weight without regaining it.

As long as you make your choices from the natural food column you are totally free to eat from each food group until you are fully satisfied.

Once you feel physical hunger (step one of the happy eating approach) all you have to do is to ask yourself two questions, 'What do I really feel like eating?' and, 'How will this food make me feel once I've eaten it?' Let's look at these two questions in turn.

Eat what you really feel like eating

When I suggest to overweight people to eat exactly what they feel like eating they often argue that this would lead them to eat even more. The answer to this argument is no - the opposite is true. The more you get what you really like, the *less* you will eat. I will explain exactly why this is so.

Why eating food that we feel like eating will lead to weight loss

Most of us overeat when we have a chance to eat

'forbidden' food (whatever that is for each person). So when we get the chance many of us can't stop ourselves and munch as much and as fast as we can. But imagine you could have this very desirable food for your next meal, the meal thereafter and then forever. What reason would there be to overeat? Exactly - none!

Some people may object at this point and argue that their favourite foods are deep-fried food and chocolate and that these foods are forbidden in the happy eating approach because they are not natural foods. But this line of thought is not quite correct. We can have *every* food in the happy eating approach as long as it is prepared with healthy ingredients. Chocolate can be replaced with a wide variety of 'chocolatey' foods if they are prepared with healthy sweeteners and cocoa powder. And deep-fried food can be prepared with a healthy fat like coconut oil. There are many cookbooks and recipe sharing sites on the internet where you can find inspiration for preparing exactly the kind of food that you feel like eating. All you have to do is replace sugar, white flour and bad fats with ingredients from the natural food columns. Healthy eating does *not* mean only eating tofu burger and green salads.

The bottom line is that in the happy eating approach you can have your favourite food at *every* mealtime *every* day and you will still lose weight if you only eat when you are hungry and keep to the natural food choices. So, if you feel like it, you can eat sweet meals every single day like pancakes, apple cake or puddings. You really can and you will still lose weight as long as these sweet dishes are prepared with wholemeal flour and a healthy sweetener and possibly with some fruit to make them more rounded nutritionally. The interesting fact is that most people's urges to overeat drastically lessen once they finally have the freedom to eat what they truly desire.

Overeating comes from depriving yourself – not from allowing yourself to follow your desires.

Here is another dynamic that leads to overeating: Many people only allow themselves their favourite food (usually a sweet dessert) once they have eaten a whole plate of 'healthy' food beforehand. As a result they eat too much and feel stuffed and bloated afterwards. No matter how nutritious their 'healthy' meal was, if the end result is overeating the whole approach leads to weight gain.

In the happy eating approach you will *only* have your favourite food and without having to eat a whole plate of supposedly healthy food beforehand.

If your favourite food is chips (french fries) with cheese, for instance, you can make the chips from fresh potatoes and fry them in coconut oil. Then you eat this meal *instead* of a whole plate of rice and meat once you feel physical hunger. The result will be that you are happy, fulfilled *and* able to lose weight. Does this make sense to you?

There is no great danger to lose out nutritionally if you eat your favourite food very often (even if it is sweet) as long as you choose it from the natural food column. The wholemeal flour, eggs, fruit and cocoa powder for a pancake meal, for instance, contain many healthy nutrients. Let me say it more dramatically: Eating junk food and being overweight will kill you. Slight nutritional deficiencies from eating too much of the same food may do you no real harm whatsoever. Interestingly, most people I have worked with naturally veered to a varied diet with many different nutrients once they felt a real freedom about their food choices. It is so simple – all we need do is to stop depriving ourselves in the wrong places.

Food has a strong impact on our mind and emotions

Many people may not be aware of the fact that food has a strong impact on our mind and emotions and that it is this impact that governs most of our food choices. Unfortunately, many diet gurus don't seem to be aware of this fact either when they tell us enthusiastically that we should 'enjoy' a breakfast of raw broccoli with pumpkin seeds or of three fried eggs topped with a teaspoon of alfalfa sprouts.

Anecdotal evidence for the emotional impact of food can be found in the way we use adjectives that describe tastes. For example, to a person we love we may say 'you are sweet' and about someone who is hardened by resentment we say 'she is bitter'. In the German language people say 'I am sour' when they mean 'I am annoyed' and we all know what it means if someone says 'she is hot'.

A more systematic approach to the impact of food on our mind can be found in the system of traditional Chinese medicine (TCM). This system is very sophisticated and the different tastes of food are used to satisfy emotional needs as well as to cure many physical imbalances. The following overview gives you an idea about how different tastes can influence our emotional and mental well-being.

The sour taste has a cooling effect on hot emotions like irritation and anger. It helps people to be more tolerant, generous and creative. On the physical level it is good for the liver and gall bladder.

The bitter taste has a relaxing effect when we feel stressed and hurried. This is probably why so many people reach for a drink of (bitter tasting) coffee, tea or a beer when they want to relax and have a break. On the physical level the bitter taste is good for the heart and small intestines.

The sweet taste calms down too much ruminating. It is grounding and enhances a feeling that 'the world is in order'. Isn't it obvious why so many people crave this taste? Most starchy carbohydrates like bread, pasta and potatoes belong to this category. On the physical level the sweet taste is good for the stomach and spleen.

The hot and spicy taste has an uplifting and activating effect on people who feel blocked or a bit depressed. On the physical level it is good for the lungs and colon.

The salty taste of savoury food strengthens confidence and courage and disperses feelings of self-pity and fear. This is why most people prefer a hearty meal before going on an adventure tour instead of something sweet.

The Chinese system also distinguishes between yin and yang food. Yang food - like meat and fried food - is activating and warming while yin food - like steamed and raw vegetables and fruit - is relaxing and cooling.

Traditional Chinese nutrition is much more sophisticated than this short overview but we can learn from it that the different tastes influence our emotional and physical states of being. However, we don't have to remember any of this because in everyday life we will know *ourselves* which taste will satisfy our emotional and physical needs simply by being aware of what we feel like eating. The good news is that our body intuitively knows what it needs and will make these needs known through our desires. Therefore, in the happy eating approach you are encouraged to simply feel inside yourself and find which taste you feel like eating. In this way you can be assured that it will be the right taste for your body and mind even if you have never heard of traditional Chinese medicine.

Knowing which food we feel like eating

You may think that it must be very easy to know which food we want to eat but I have seen with my clients that this is not necessarily the case. Here is a script of a conversation that I had with a client about just this issue.

> *'I'm going through a deep emotional crisis' my client said, 'and all your advice about eating has gone out of the window. I'm afraid I'm back to eating shop-bought biscuits and cake all day. I just need some comfort right now.'*
>
> *'I quite understand', I said, 'and you should have some comfort food at this difficult time. Let's see if we can find some natural food alternatives to the cake and biscuits you're eating.' I knew from previous conversations with my client that she would never make the time or effort to bake her own cake from healthy ingredients. Therefore I suggested, 'why don't you have some wholemeal crispbread with butter and agave syrup instead. That is sweet and crispy just like a biscuit and should bring some comfort.' Unfortunately, my client didn't know what a crispbread was. 'What about a wholemeal muesli with grapes and some cream to make it more filling?' I ventured.*
>
> *'What?' my client exclaimed, 'I thought cream is bad for you!'*
>
> *'Saturated fat is not the best fat', I replied, 'but it is certainly a whole lot better than the hydrogenated fat that you're eating in your biscuits. The*

French use cream at every opportunity and they have less heart disease or obesity than most other Western countries. The low-fat gurus find that very annoying but the French are happy.'

'Muesli with cream', my client said with relish. 'I think I'd like that. But in my wildest dreams I would never have thought of that. Why don't you write about this in your book? For me the only form of comfort food is junk food. I was entirely unaware that you could eat something that's comforting that's not junk food.'

'I take your point', I said to my client and that was how the dialogue found its way into this book.

A major problem with food choices is that most of us are very repetitive and always eat the same things. Therefore, I would like to encourage you to look around in your supermarket to discover new and inspiring foods. If you still don't have any idea what you want to eat you can go through some or all of the following questions.

***Would** I like to have something sweet or savoury?*

***Would** I like something hot or cold?*

***Would** I like something crunchy or soft?*

***Would** I like something spicy or mild?*

***Would** I like something rich or light?*

As I have said before, sweet food is totally acceptable in the happy eating approach and you can have it as often as you desire. For example, you could eat wholemeal breakfast cereals with fruit for breakfast, lunch or dinner if this is what you like. You could also lightly steam apples or pears and eat them with brown sticky rice, butter and a healthy sweetener.

The more you get your food choices right, the more likely you will feel satisfied after a meal *and stay that way for several hours*. But if you force yourself to eat a crunchy salad with fish when you would have much rather eaten a soft food like spaghetti and tomato sauce, you are much more likely to overeat or raid your biscuit tin shortly afterwards. Therefore, it is essential that you always choose the tastes you feel like eating and have fat, protein and carbohydrates in the quantities that are most satisfying for *you*. You can trust that your choices will lead to optimal weight loss.

Can I really eat as much fat as I desire?

The short answer to this question is yes. The long answer is – eat as much fat as you need to feel truly satisfied but not more. We need fat in many ways but we don't need it in excessive amounts.

Let's first look at why we need fat. If you have ever tried a very low-fat diet you probably know how intensely dissatisfying it is. The food tastes bland, dry and leaves us with constant cravings. These cravings are actually a healthy response to a deficient diet. Nutritionists have explained that if we eat too little fat our gall bladder stops working properly and doesn't squeeze out enough bile to digest all the food that we eat in its place. The result is bloating and undigested food rotting in our intestines giving us a multitude of negative symptoms. In addition, without an appropriate amount of fat we can't digest Vitamins A, D, E, or K, which will leave us malnourished in the long-term. It has also been observed that very low-fat diets can cause or aggravate depression, fluid retention, fatigue, allergies, yeast infections and PMS.

On the other hand, it is fat that makes food tasty because it enhances flavour and gives it that special 'yum-yum' ingredient. Healthy fats are good not only for our taste buds but also for our body and – believe or not – for weight loss because it stops us overeating carbohydrates in the search of that special satisfaction that only fat can provide. Therefore, we should *not* try to eat a low-fat diet in the happy eating approach.

On the other hand, we should not use excessive amounts, either. 'But how much fat is a moderate amount?' you may ask. You can find the answer yourself by noticing which amount of fat makes *you* feel satisfied. We are all different and what is enough for one person may not be enough for another. If you suspect that you eat too much fat, try cutting it down to half and see how you feel. If your food starts tasting bland and dissatisfying you will have to add some fat back into your diet. After experimenting with this for a little while you will quickly find out which amount of fat is right for you. By using healthy fats you won't need to worry that every fat gram will make you fat. Quite the contrary, the weight loss promoting faculties of these oils are real and you should not underestimate them. Here is a personal story that exemplifies this point:

> *Many years ago I went to a naturopath because of a health complaint and he insisted that I had to eat a very low-fat diet in order to get better. At first I was sceptical because it was one of my principles never to fiddle with what my body told me to eat. However, I was also intrigued to see if the advice of the naturopath would improve my health. So I decided to give it a try.*
>
> *I continued to eat in exactly the same way as I had done before – natural food when I was hungry and stopped when I was full – but I cut out virtually all fat. In this way my calorie intake must have gone considerably down because I stuck to more or less the same portion sizes as before.*
>
> *Paradoxically, my weight went up and within two weeks I had gained an amazing five pounds. This was highly unusual as my weight had always been very stable. Obviously, I wasn't best pleased and as my health hadn't*

> *improved one little bit I went back to my old way of eating which was more on the high-fat side. Within two weeks my weight returned to normal.*

My experience is not exceptional and over the years I have talked to other people who gained weight on low-fat diets. What we can learn from these experiences is this: it is crucial to listen to what our body tells us. If our body craves fat then this fat may actually be what we need. Our body always has the option to store excess calories as fat or burn them as fuel. In some people healthy fats enable the body to do the latter.

What about carbohydrates – won't they make me fat?

There are only two sorts of carbohydrate that will make you fat and they are refined white flour and sugar. It is unfortunate that the low-carb craze often lumps all carbohydrates into one category implying that they are all bad. Nothing could be further from the truth. Scientist Linda van Horn conducted a study which included 4000 people from China, Japan, Great Britain and the USA. She found that *without exception* the slimmest people in each society ate a diet high in complex carbohydrate and vegetable protein (as in grains, legumes and soy). By comparison, high-protein diets were associated with higher body weight.

You don't need to take this on trust, you can gather proof yourself by looking for people you know who have eaten for years a diet high in complex carbohydrates while shunning sugar and other convenience food. I personally don't know a single person who has done this and has excess weight. Therefore, if you like carbohydrates you can have them in any amount that will make you feel good. You can rest assured that you are simply following the tradition of many natural societies whose members keep slim throughout their life and rarely develop degenerative diseases. In addition, you can fully relish the happy feeling that comes from no other food like it does from carbohydrates. And remember, the more you can enjoy your meals the less you will overeat. Don't you feel like eating a bowl of spaghetti or some crusty rolls? Please, don't allow anyone to tell you that you can't have them.

If you are one of those people who never eats fruit and vegetables, I would like to encourage you to experiment with adding some of these foods into your diet. Without them even the happy eating approach might become a bit deficient over time. Fried chicken with french fries from a fast-food outlet might taste good on its own but freshly cooked chicken with potatoes is calling for something more. It wants some peas, carrots or a salad on its side to be really tasty. Try it, you might be pleasantly surprised. I am not asking you to subsist on salads or fruit cocktails – just adding *some* veggies and fruits to most of your meals will give you everything you need to have a nutritionally complete diet. You can start very simply by adding some slices of cucumber or tomato to your sandwich or you could dice up an onion to cook with your meat.

How much protein should I eat in the happy eating approach?

When it comes to protein the experts disagree as wildly as they do in most other areas of nutrition. Therefore I recommend what I have done before: let your body be the ultimate diet guru and eat as much protein as you feel like eating and makes you feel good in the hours after you've eaten it. Just make sure that you choose high quality protein from organic meat, fish, dairy or vegetable sources.

Generally speaking, protein is every dieter's best friend because it is the most satiating food. This means that a meal with a good amount of protein (between 10 and 20 grams) will make you feel full far longer than a meal consisting only of carbohydrates and fat. Remember, the more satisfaction and long-term satiety you get from your food, the less you will need to eat and the more weight you will lose. I encourage everyone to try this out and then to adjust the amount of protein in your diet so that it feels best and gives you most satiety.

Eating a good amount of protein doesn't necessarily mean eating lots of meat or eggs. You can obtain the most condensed amount of protein from various protein powders, which can be added to drinks and food, for example in sauces, cakes and on top of breakfast cereals. (I admit that these are highly processed foods but for the purpose of getting enough protein into your diet they can be very useful.)

There are various forms of protein powders, for example from soy, hemp or peas. My own favourite protein powder is whey, which is a by-product of making cheese. In centuries past, whey was hailed as a form of miracle cure and there were many special spas all over Europe that dispensed this amazing food to the rich and famous who were the only ones who could afford this product that usually spoiled within hours. However, nowadays everybody can afford whey protein through the technique of freeze drying. Gunter A. Ulmer describes in his book *The Newly Discovered Healthy Whey* (translated from the German) the amazing health benefits of whey, which are mainly achieved through its detoxifying effect on the body. In addition, whey contains many important nutrients and minerals.

Adding protein powders to your drinks and sipping them throughout the day will ward off hunger and can therefore make it a lot easier to keep to the rules of the happy eating approach and lose weight. But I certainly do not recommend trying to replace meals with protein drinks as many popular diets recommend. Doing this would bring you back onto the roller coaster ride of deprivation and bingeing and that is the opposite of what we want to achieve. Protein drinks that you sip throughout the day are just a nifty little trick to make everything in the happy eating approach a bit easier simply because you will be less hungry.

However, it is by no means necessary to use protein drinks to achieve a healthy weight with the happy eating approach. Even without this help my clients were able to get to the healthy weight range and so can you!

Eat what makes you feel good after you have eaten it

Now we will be looking more closely at the effects that your food has on your mind and body *after* you have eaten it. Generally speaking, the better you can digest your food the better your overall health will be and the better your body will be able to ward off excess fat. On the other hand, if you experience bloating, tiredness and indigestion on a regular basis your body isn't coping well with the fuel you are feeding it. The food will lie rotting in your intestines producing gas and toxins that will in turn cause physical ailments. Instead of efficiently turning food calories into energy and warmth, you will feel tired, ailing and – fat.

Good digestion is the key to well-being, health and weight loss.

In many cases the food that you feel like eating will also make you feel good afterwards but unfortunately, this is not always the case. For example, you may feel like eating a jacket potato but the potato may not feel like being eaten by you and will give you terrible bloating afterwards. Or you may feel like eating an egg but it makes you feel slightly nauseous.

You should only eat food that you feel like eating *and* that makes you feel good after you have eaten it.

Following this guideline should not be too difficult because I am only asking you to maximise your well-being – and that's something everybody wants to do anyway. Therefore, you need to pay attention to how food makes you feel in the hours after you have eaten it.

Possible symptoms to look out for are bloating, tiredness, flatulence, burping, nausea or heartburn. Sometimes you may even experience a reoccurrence of old physical symptoms after eating certain foods. For example, some people get a runny nose as soon as they eat a dairy product.

Dealing with digestive discomfort

In the following paragraphs we will look at the most common digestive discomforts and what we can do about these problems.

Bloating and tiredness: The most common discomfort people experience after eating is an uncomfortable feeling of being bloated and tired. It is of paramount importance to get rid of these symptoms because tiredness and bloating not only make us *feel* fat they will *literally make* us fat. As I have explained before, our body always has the option of storing excess calories as fat or burning them for more energy. If we feel tired and bloated after a meal our body is clearly not going for the energy option. Simply put, our body can't deal with digestive problems and burn calories effectively at the same time.

The easiest way to minimise bloating and tiredness after a meal is to not overeat and to chew properly. This common sense advice can improve our digestion in amazing ways and will be discussed in more detail in enjoyable step four.

If your indigestion continues despite these simple measures it is a sign that your digestive organs are overtaxed. Your liver may be congested, your pancreas may release too much insulin or your intestines may be ineffective because of a fungal infection like Candida. All these symptoms can be caused or aggravated through a diet high in sugar, white flour or low-quality fat. Whatever the precise cause, if you can't digest your food properly you are likely to store it as fat instead of burning it off as fuel.

Therefore, in order to get rid of bloating and tiredness you need to find the offending food and cut it out for some time. Often you will find that you can reintroduce this food once you have had a little rest from it. For a great many people the culprits are too many starchy carbohydrates like sugar, grain products and potatoes. This happens particularly often if their digestive organs have been overworked through the consumption of too much sugary food and white flour in the past.

If you suffer from bloating and tiredness after a meal I suggest that you try eating your source of protein (e.g. meat, eggs or soy) with some vegetables without any pasta, bread or potatoes and see what happens. If your indigestion gets better, rejoice because you will feel a lot better and you will probably lose weight quite fast, as well. But let me stress that the happy eating approach is not a low-carb diet in disguise. You can always eat as many carbohydrates as you are able to tolerate. You may find, for example, that you can tolerate two slices of toast in the morning but the same amount of bread or pasta in the evening makes you feel very uncomfortable. Then, simply eat non-bloating vegetables, instead.

Cutting out sugar and white flour will also benefit anyone who suffers from a fungal infection like Candida as this fungus feeds on the glucose in these foods. I myself suffered from Candida for many years and I noticed that the big turnaround happened for me when I cut out sugar and starches for a while and used coconut oil as my primary source of fat. Coconut oil has antifungal, antiviral and antibacterial properties and is an important factor in getting rid of Candida for good.

The good news is that most people have to cut out starches for only a limited time. So, once you feel a yearning for some bread – go ahead and have some. If it doesn't make you tired or bloated it won't make you fat. You can simply allow yourself to be guided by what makes you feel good and you will lose your weight without any deprivation. It's easy – don't you think?

If you find that you get bloated or tired with or

without starchy carbohydrates, you will have to investigate dairy products. Many people don't do that well on milk and cheese and if it bloats them, it is more likely to make them fat. Some unfortunate souls will find that they can't tolerate dairy or starchy carbohydrates. If you are one of them you need to experiment with eating vegetables with eggs, meat or soy in the morning. It may feel strange at first but it if you feel better afterwards you might do it quite happily.

Remember, however, that all this cutting out of food groups is necessary only as long as it makes you feel better. As soon as you find that you can tolerate starchy carbohydrates and dairy, you can add them back into your diet even if you still have some weight to lose.

Another form of bloating is caused by pulses and foods like cabbage and cucumber which produce lots of gas in the process of digestion. Luckily, this problem can be alleviated by rinsing your beans and lentils more thoroughly (seven times, to be precise) and by adding caraway seed or dill weed to your cabbage and cucumber dishes.

Nausea: Slight nausea can be a sign of having eaten too much fat or a low-quality fat. As you will remember, in the happy eating approach it is recommended that you eat a moderate amount of healthy fat. But please don't get obsessive about your fat intake. It is by no means necessary to know about fat grams, calories and the like. Just avoid junk food fat, learn roughly how much healthy fat you need and don't eat a lot more or less.

Another reason for nausea is an individual intolerance for certain foods like fish or eggs, for example. As it has been explained before, you need to find the offending food by being aware of how it makes you feel after you have eaten it. Then you can cut it out and see if your well-being improves. Once your body has had a rest from a difficult food it will often heal and you may find that you can tolerate this food to a certain degree later on.

Heartburn: This is a pain behind the breastbone caused by involuntarily regurgitated food and it is often caused or aggravated by stress or by eating too much food too fast. In the happy eating approach you are encouraged to enjoy all aspects of food - starting from going shopping and buying what inspires you, preparing your food with love and eating it with relish. Eating on the run and under time pressure diminishes these joys and encourages weight gain because it is bad for your health. In order to alleviate heartburn you need to really enjoy your food, eat slowly, chew well and stop at the first sign of fullness. Drinking a large glass of water at the first sign of heartburn often helps as well.

If you often suffer from heartburn, it can be very beneficial to eat at other times than your children. Family meals are often romanticised – in reality they are all too often fraught with stress because for some mysterious reason many children choose to misbehave just at these times.

In many cases making some of the simple changes

outlined above will be enough to remedy your digestive problems. However, some unfortunate people will find that they have many different food intolerances. If you are one of them it can be very helpful to write a food diary and jot down which food has what effect on you. It is also beneficial to go to a doctor or naturopath in order to heal and strengthen your inner organs. Bear in mind though that ordinary Western medicine has little to offer in terms of curing mild digestive problems. Also, be wary of over-the-counter remedies that are just masking the symptoms. Real help for the symptoms from above can only be expected from herbalists, nutritionists and naturopaths because they can get to the underlying cause of persistent indigestion and are able to eliminate it permanently.

Imagine how a food will make you feel after a meal

Once you have thought of a food that you feel like eating you should ask yourself, 'How will this food make me feel once I have eaten it?' For instance, imagine you want to eat a bowl of pasta and now try to guess how you would feel after you have eaten the pasta. If you get a feeling of some sort of indigestion or bloating, pasta would not be the right food for you right now and it would be better to try something else.

After you have thought of another food ask yourself again how this food would make you feel after you have eaten it and try to imagine its effect. If you can imagine eating a certain food without any discomfort afterwards then you can go ahead and enjoy it.

Cutting out food that will give you digestive discomfort and thus makes you fat is amazingly easy. Once you realise how bad you will feel after certain foods you will hardly need any self-discipline to let them go. You don't need to be told by a diet guru that certain foods are bad for you but you will cut them out voluntarily and *by your own choice*. Doing this is greatly empowering and is one of the major reasons why people are successful in the happy eating approach but fail on other diets. One client of mine put it quite aptly:

> *'Tara', she said, 'these potato crisps are looking at me. They've been looking at me for days. But I know that if I eat them it will be over in one minute and afterwards I'll feel bloated and awful for hours. It simply isn't worth it. In the past I never asked myself how a food will make me feel after I've eaten it and always succumbed to all the temptations around me. But if I ask this question it makes it so much easier to stay away from fattening food.'*

Many people are astonished how well they can intuit how a certain food will make them feel once they have eaten it. However, sometimes you may find that a certain food that you thought you could digest well doesn't agree with you. In that case you need to make a (mental) note about the offending food and cut it out for a little while.

Eat the food that you feel like eating - and only that

This is an important rule because it simplifies what we can eat and what we can't. It is really very simple – eat the dish that you feel like eating and stop there. Do not eat meals with several courses (at least not a regular basis) because it is very easy to overeat. Eating one-course meals will be very easy if you have chosen a food that you feel like eating. Why would you want to eat another course when you have already had what you desired most?

By contrast, if you find yourself craving a dessert after eating a full meal something is wrong. Probably, you didn't allow yourself to choose the food that you *really* desired because you may still be hemmed in by the power of the diet gurus. You might not have dared, for instance, to add enough fat to your meal or you might have been mean with the carbohydrates. As a result, you may feel dissatisfied after a meal and crave a fatty pudding to make up for your unnecessary self-deprivation. Or maybe you simply didn't eat enough. For each of these cases I would like to encourage you to eat the food that you *really* feel like eating in the quantities that fill you up.

If you feel like eating a sweet meal, for example, please feel free to have it first thing – and only that - and don't eat a whole 'healthy' meal beforehand. It has been drummed into most of us that we need to eat certain foods at every mealtime and that we can only have a dessert if we eat it all up. The end result will be that we eat too many calories. I promise you that you will feel so much happier if you let go of these unnecessary restrictions.

If you are invited to a special three-course meal, please feel free to enjoy it but be aware that the number of calories ingested on these occasions are enormous. For many of my clients it comes as a surprise that they don't need another morsel for a very long time after such a sumptuous lunch.

Frequently asked questions for enjoyable step three

'I find it hard to trust that I will get the appropriate nutrients by eating only food that I desire.'

If you keep to the natural food column and allow yourself to follow your inner impulses you will find that your desires will lead you exactly to what you need. If you are short on iron, for example, you may find yourself craving meat. Or if you lack potassium you may suddenly feel like eating bananas. Our bodies are excellent nutritionists if we allow them to be in charge. One client told me, for instance, how she suddenly found herself craving large glasses of milk even though she had never drank a lot of milk before. It was not by coincidence that she was postmenopausal and suffered from a slow to heal bone injury. Her body showed her through its craving that it needed more calcium.

'I hardly feel like eating carbohydrates. Should I force myself?'

Please don't! If you include some tasty vegetables in your diet and otherwise eat what you feel like eating, you will ingest the amount of nutrients that is right for you.

'Why don't you supply some recipes for the happy eating approach?'

If you are looking for recipes take any cookbook that inspires you and replace any unhealthy ingredients with wholemeal products, healthy fats and sweeteners. Many diet books come with very precise day-to-day plans prescribing what and how much to eat. Unfortunately, these plans are really beside the point because the dietary needs of different people vary so vastly. One client of mine, for example, *gained* weight when she was on the regime of a slimming club even though she didn't cheat. After she was told off in front of the whole group, she stopped going.

It's the beauty and freedom of the happy eating approach that you can eat anything and everything in the quantities you desire as long as you follow your hunger signals and keep away from junk food. You can trust that your body naturally wants to be slim as much as it naturally wants to be healthy.

'The government recommends five portions of fruit and vegetables a day but I feel like eating only three. What should I do?'

In my humble opinion the government should be concerned with governing the country and not telling people what to eat. Just because this advice comes from the government doesn't mean that it is any more true than the contradictory advice of dozens of diet gurus. The ultimate diet guru is your own body and if you are happiest with three pieces of fruit and vegetables a day – please enjoy them and don't worry.

Pitfalls for enjoyable step three

'I often can't find the food that I feel like eating so I have to go shopping first and starve in the meantime.'

Please don't starve yourself. If you are hungry and you can't get hold of a proper meal eat something small like a banana, some nuts or half a slice of bread until you can get your desired food. When you go shopping make sure that you buy a variety of food that you like and that will last for a few days. As time goes by you will know better what and how much you need to never go hungry.

'I had to throw away lots of food I bought because I didn't feel like eating it when it came to mealtime.'

Only put in your shopping trolley what you really

feel like eating. Once you prepare your food at home make sure you eat *roughly* what you like – there is no need to become rigid about any of the rules of the happy eating approach.

'I find it hard to forget all the diet advice that I have accumulated over the years.'

Did this diet advice make you happy, healthy and slim? If yes, then stick to it. But if this diet advice made you feel deprived, guilt-ridden and unable to lose weight then I suggest that you try something new. Many, many people have lost weight with the happy eating approach. As I have explained before, it is the way that slim people eat naturally and you have nothing to lose by giving it a try as well. Here is a little story that demonstrates this point:

> *One client of mine told me with admiration about an eighty year old lady she knows who was remarkably slim and fit. My client had a conversation with this lady to try to find out the secret of her good health and trim figure. She told me that every day this old lady would go into her kitchen, open her cupboard and look into her fridge and ask herself, 'what would I feel like eating today?' 'Yes', I said, waiting for some interesting information but my client's story had already ended. The old lady's 'secret' was to eat what she fancied and for my client this was a major revelation.*

What to do if you fail to follow enjoyable step three

First of all, be kind to yourself and send love to yourself with the exercise explained at the end of step one. The more love you can send to yourself with all your problems and weaknesses, the more quickly you will be able to put your positive resolutions into practice.

You are bound to fail on enjoyable step three and there is nothing wrong with that. On the contrary, it can be greatly liberating to gradually learn to identify the food that is causing you discomfort and to be able to do something about it. This process will take time for most people and you shouldn't worry about that.

One way of speeding up this process is to write a food diary and make a note of the effect your food has on your body and mind. When I was 22 years old I wrote such a diary for one entire year. This may seem like a long time but I am still benefiting from the insights that I gained then.

Once you know which food causes your bloating and digestive discomfort it will be quite easy to give it up because nobody voluntary does something that will make them suffer. At the end of the book you will find a sample page showing how to write a food diary. The example is a very detailed one and you can copy it the way it is or adjust it and simplify it to your liking.

The bottom line for enjoyable step three

Choose a dish that you really feel like eating, no matter whether this is ordinarily considered a dessert, a breakfast or a starter. Just make sure that this food has been prepared with natural ingredients.

Before you start preparing the food ask yourself how it will make you feel once you have eaten it. If you can imagine eating it without any discomfort you can go ahead and enjoy it. If you cannot imagine that, choose something else.

Eat your most desired food and only that. Do not add other courses to this meal.

Affirmations for enjoyable step three

If a food makes me feel really good, it will help me to lose weight.

The more I eat exactly what I feel like eating, the more weight I will lose.

Enjoyable step four
Eat as much as you enjoy

Isn't this another attractive step? 'Yes', you might say, 'but doesn't it open the gate for people to binge?' The answer is no because noone truly *enjoys* bingeing. If you don't believe me, you can try it out. Next time you catch yourself in a binge try positively to enjoy every morsel of it. Really relish each bite and stop immediately once the feeling of enjoyment is replaced by a sense of uncomfortable fullness, guilt, disgust or repulsion. The truth is that we can only overeat while being relatively unaware of what the food is doing to our body and mind. But as soon as we insist that we want to enjoy every morsel of our food, the binge will be often over very quickly.

Let me give you example of this intriguing dynamic from my own life. When I was a teenager and in my early twenties, I used to smoke. Once I had lost all my excess weight with the principles of the happy eating approach I wanted to give up smoking, too. But in the course of learning to enjoy all my food I developed a strong repulsion to force myself in any way. Therefore, simply denying myself the cigarettes was not an option for me. Instead, I gave myself one simple rule which was 'I have to enjoy every lungful of smoke or else I have to extinguish the cigarette immediately'. The results of this guideline were quite dramatic.

I noticed that I enjoyed rolling the tobacco into thin

cigarettes and the first two puffs were enjoyable as well. But then I made some shocking observations. The more puffs I took the colder my legs and arms would become often leaving me shivering and with an uncomfortable feeling of having no blood in my extremities. Simultaneously, I would start to feel slightly nauseous and more often than not a feeling of mild depression would set in. Boy, did I extinguish that cigarette quickly!

Interestingly, I had vaguely known about all these negative consequences of smoking before but my insights had mostly stayed in my semi-conscious mind because I didn't pay attention to them. When I fully faced the impact of smoking on my mind and body, most of my desire to smoke simply disappeared. Within three days I was down to two or three cigarettes a day from which I only took a few puffs. A few weeks later I suddenly noticed that I hadn't smoked for at least three days. So, in fact, I had given up smoking without even noticing it.

Coming back to eating, you can employ exactly the same guideline and simply insist that you *have to* really enjoy every morsel of your food or else stop eating. The happy eating approach is all about learning to enjoy food and eating. All the steps of the happy eating approach are designed to maximise your enjoyment. Here is a small re-cap of how to derive more pleasure and happiness from everything to do with food, eating and diet:

Enjoyable step one instructed us to eat in line with our physical hunger which will make even the simplest meals taste delicious. As an additional side-effect, worries and guilt-feelings about eating will disappear, too.

Enjoyable step two encouraged us to give up junk food that will make us feel bloated, sick and ultimately kill us. Instead we were asked to eat wholesome, fresh and natural food that will give us energy with the additional satisfaction that comes from being good to ourselves and the people we are cooking for.

In enjoyable step three we were instructed only to eat what we really feel like eating and to stay away from diet food or anything that will give us digestive discomfort and other ailments.

Now, in enjoyable step four we come to the actual process of eating and I will show you how to maximise the enjoyment of doing it.

It is really weird that in our society of food abundance so few people are actually able to fully enjoy what has been given to them. Many overweight people eat with constant guilt and fear which robs them of all the joy. As a result they eat even more to find the elusive satisfaction that slim people have. But many naturally slim people know that eating junk food and overeating doesn't feel that good. You can only do it if you ignore the signals of your body and override feelings of uncomfortable bloating, repulsion and even disgust. Therefore, the first step to stop overeating is to insist that you *must* enjoy every morsel.

Relishing every morsel of food will make you slim

At some point in my happy eating approach groups I always bring in a plate with small bits of tasty food. I invite everybody to have a piece or two and to pay close attention to how it feels to eat this food in front of the group. Can you guess how much people enjoy this process? It is sad but most group members don't enjoy this process at all. This is not because I bring in bland and yucky diet food (in fact, they might be able to enjoy diet food a little bit more). No, people feel guilt-ridden, self-conscious and ashamed for the simple reason that they might be seen enjoying yummy food. I never tried this exercise with a group of naturally slim people but I am sure that they would be able to relish those same morsels a lot more.

You may now be saying that the people in my groups can't enjoy this food because they are fat. But I am saying the opposite:

People are fat because they can't enjoy their food.

If people could enjoy their food they would prefer to eat when they hungry, they would stop eating unsatisfying diet food or sickening junk food and they would never overeat. In short, they would be like all those self-satisfied slim people who proclaim that they can eat anything they like. Therefore, if you want to lose weight you need to learn the high art of actually relishing every bite that you eat. Because this is so difficult for most overweight people I will give you a few guidelines:

A first experience of consciously relishing a bite of food

I would like to invite you to try a little experiment and it is preferable that you choose a time when you are undisturbed. Then you can go into your kitchen and look for a bite to eat – anything that you feel like eating. It could be a piece of fruit, a morsel of bread with butter or a piece of cheese. You can choose but make sure you find something really yummy.

Before you eat this morsel please look at it and anticipate its delicious taste. Feel the enjoyment that arises from your anticipation. In the next step, smell your food and really relish this experience. Let the pleasant sensation of smelling the food pervade your entire body. When you breathe out, do it with a deeply enjoyable 'mmmmhhh'. Do this one or two more times and notice how saliva gathers in your mouth and how your whole being joyfully anticipates the pleasant experience that will follow.

Put a small morsel of the food into your mouth and before you start chewing let your tongue and your taste buds embrace this food. Suck at it a little bit, lick it lightly and feel the texture and a first glimpse of its taste. Again, relish this experience with a deeply enjoyable 'mmmmmhhh' and let it pervade all through your body.

Now start to chew very slowly. Feel the consistency

of the food; notice whether it is soft or crunchy and feel how its taste starts to pervade your mouth. Roll the food from one side of your mouth to the other giving all your taste buds a chance to relish its wonderful taste. Carry on deepening your enjoyment by making more noises like 'mmmmmhhh' and let the pleasure of your experience spread all over your being. Notice how your mouth releases more and more saliva to produce a highly delicious mush in your mouth.

Don't swallow just yet. Carry on a little longer to relish your morsel until it is entirely liquid. Then swallow.

How do you feel now? Was it nice? Do you realise that you could have this delightful experience every day dozens of times? No, hundreds of times, actually. It is simply a matter of paying attention. If you feel guilty for having experienced so much pleasure, remember that there are no moral, religious or social rules that say that we mustn't relish our food. We are entirely entitled to this experience and we can have it as often as we like. Obviously, when other people are present you might want to keep the 'mmmmhhh' a little bit down. However, I encourage you not to forget it altogether and, socially, it is completely acceptable to say it once in a while.

Getting more enjoyment from your food by eating slowly

Would you enjoy a movie in fast forward mode?

Would you like to have a hurried massage or sexual intercourse that lasts 30 seconds? Of course you don't because you would like to enjoy all these things. The key to enjoying food is the same – don't hurry, sit down and eat slowly with relish. Remember, doing this will help you to become slim.

If you get more enjoyment out of your food you will be satisfied with less. It is the unconscious wolfing down of food while working at your computer or watching the telly that leads to obesity. When 90% of our attention is on the computer or on the telly we will get only 10% of possible enjoyment from what we eat. As a result we will tend to eat a lot more than we need because we are still craving satisfaction from our food. Therefore:

It is very important to sit down for every meal at a properly laid table and slowly relish our food without being distracted.

At first sight this advice may sound like deprivation because it is a little bit more work to lay a table but I believe that once you try this out, you will notice that this tiny bit of effort is well worth it. After all, you are learning to be really kind to yourself and allowing yourself more pleasure around food than you ever had before. For many people in my happy eating approach groups, laying a table feels like a positive change in their life.

When you start eating make sure that you are taking your time. Between every mouthful put down your fork or your sandwich and relish the taste and the texture in your mouth - chewing every morsel in your mouth until it has transformed into a mush.

Chewing your food properly will make you slim

There is an old saying that goes, 'Well chewed is half digested'. This saying is literally true. While we are mixing the food in our mouth with saliva, enzymes are released that already start to digest the carbohydrates. The more we can pre-digest carbohydrates in this way, the easier they will be assimilated into our body and symptoms like bloating and tiredness can be reduced to a minimum or eliminated entirely.

All food that is transformed into a thin mush in our mouth will be digested much more easily. Imagine how hard our body will have to work if we swallow large chunks of protein or carbohydrates. It will take hours and hours for the stomach and intestines to do what our teeth could do within minutes. During all these hours the undigested food will sit in our tummy at relatively high temperature – and will start to rot. This rotting process is one of the reasons for bloating and tiredness after a meal because it is a great strain on the body. In addition to the extra digestive work our intestines have to do, our body also has to deal with all the toxins that are created in this rotting process instead of concentrating on its main task which is transforming food into energy. The end result will of course be either weight gain or the slowing down of our weight loss.

Eliminating junk food and chewing our food properly are the most important steps to help

our body to burn food as fuel rather than storing it as fat.

You don't have to count how often you chew each morsel because this would not be enjoyable and therefore goes against the principles of the happy eating approach. But I do encourage you to chew each mouthful of food until it is a yummy mush. You should also do this with soft food like pasta because you will be minimising the danger of having indigestion afterwards. Try it out with a food that will normally give you a lot of uncomfortable bloating. You may very well be pleasantly surprised.

Chewing your food is such a common sense advice that many people will read it and forget it again the next minute. But please don't forget this advice and the next paragraph will give you some more – almost shocking - evidence showing that chewing your food more thoroughly really can make you slim.

How people lose their weight after having weight loss surgery

During weight loss surgery the stomach of an obese person is made into a much smaller receptacle and has an 80% success rate in helping people to lose weight. Do you know why? It's not because people will have to starve because of their tiny stomachs. After all, weight loss surgery patients are very well able to maintain a healthy weight for the rest of their life. This surgery helps people to lose weight because it forces them to chew their food more thoroughly – or else they will vomit. The following guidelines are taken from a website of a weight loss surgery clinic in New York. They say that after weight loss surgery...

You'll have to change your eating and exercise pattern...

Eat slowly and chew your foods until they are mushy...

Aim for 30 chews for each bite, chewing thoroughly to a mush...

Take small bites...

Savour each bite, noting its taste, flavour and texture

Sit down and be focused on eating, not on other activities where you can become distracted

Stop eating as soon as you feel full. If you eat too much you'll get sick.

When you get a feeling of fullness, stop eating, even if you have not finished your meal

Set aside three meals a day when you only eat solid foods. This will help you to eat nutritious meals rather than endless snacking. Snacking could prevent you from losing weight. It could even cause you to gain weight...

What you are going to eat needs to be high quality and packed with nutrients...

Don't you think that the advice of the weight-surgery clinic is very reminiscent of the happy eating approach? Basically, weight loss surgery is no more a magic bullet than any other weight loss programme. It all boils down to eating high-quality food slowly when you are hungry and stopping when you are full. The happy eating approach helps you to ease into this pattern by noticing how enjoyable it is and weight loss surgery forces you by giving you lots of pain and nausea if you stray. I know which path I prefer.

Chewing your food more properly can result in astounding weight loss. People find they are satisfied with less food, they get hungry less often and they feel and become slimmer even if they eat to their full satisfaction. I once watched a show on television in which they tried an experiment. They had three groups of people in a weight loss clinic so that they could make sure nobody was cheating. The first group were given a low calorie diet, the second group was given a low carb/high-protein diet and the last group could eat what they wanted but had to chew their food 30 times with each mouthful. This was called the 'chew-chew diet' which apparently was already popular in the UK a hundred years ago.

All the people were eating all their meals together and it was especially hard for the people on the low calorie diet to have to look on to the people from third group tucking into cake and other yummy food while they were served only salads and similar foods.

You can probably guess why I am telling you about this experiment at this point because the people on the chew-chew diet lost a lot more weight than the people on both the low calorie and the low-carb diets, even though – and this is even more amazing – they consumed a lot more calories. Unfortunately, I did not note the name of this program so that you could watch it on the internet, so you will have to take my word for it. But I have this account from one of my slim friends who suffered from frequent bloating, which proves the same point:

> *I remember being told to chew more thoroughly in the past. It's such a common sense advice but being a working mother all this multi-tasking meant I was constantly eating in front of the computer or on the run. Looking back it's no surprise that I had all this indigestion.*
>
> *Once I started chewing more thoroughly several things happened. First of all, my digestion improved. When I got up from the table I could hardly feel that I just had eaten a full meal. Secondly, I ate a bit less than I used to. My mealtimes lasted longer than before but I often ate only three quarters of what I have eaten before. Thirdly – and this is really surprising – my food lasted longer even though I had eaten less. Fourthly, I lost weight even though I wasn't overweight.*

Stop when you feel 100% satisfied

Like all other 'rules' in the happy eating approach this advice focuses on finding the ideal amount of food by maximising the enjoyment you get out of eating. Here is how it works: At your next meal I invite you to try a little experiment and rate your satisfaction while you eat. After your first bite, for example, you may feel 5% satisfied. After you have been half way through your meal you may feel 50% satisfied. Silently count in this way while paying full attention to the enjoyment of eating as we discussed earlier. Focus on satisfaction rather than only on feeling full because the latter is a purely physical experience while satisfaction encompasses your body *and* your mind. And in the happy eating approach we are always trying to cater for both your body and your emotions.

As you come near to 80% satisfaction you should pay extra attention so as not to miss 100%. Try to focus on your stomach and not only on your mouth. You don't want to overshoot because 110% would mean an uncomfortable feeling of fullness. In order to stop eating when you are 100% satisfied you have to be mindful and fully concentrate on your enjoyment. You will quickly notice that when you overeat your enjoyment gradually lessens and turns into a sense of uncomfortable fullness or even bloating. You will also notice that the taste of the food becomes blander and more dissatisfying. You may even feel a sense of repulsion for the very food that you relished just one minute ago.

The aim is to stop eating when you feel 100%

satisfied or very near to that mark. You don't want to get up from the table with lingering cravings and you don't want to feel overly full either.

Ideally, after a meal you should feel light, energetic and fully satisfied.

You don't have to rate your satisfaction in this way for all your meals but it is always a good idea to try to catch the moment when you are 80% satisfied. After that you should slow down your eating even further so that you can comfortably stop when you are at 100%.

In the beginning you will probably find that you may inadvertently overshoot or leave the table with lingering cravings. This should not worry you because if you are still hungry you can simply go back to the table and eat some more. If you have overeaten you don't need to worry, either. Simply wait for your next physical hunger, which will probably be an hour or two later than usual. In many cases this will take care of occasional overeating. However, the ideal is to be 100% satisfied because our organism burns fat at the highest rate when it is not overworked. Also, it will feel so much better!

If you have trouble in determining your level of fullness and satisfaction, here is a simple method that can make things a little bit clearer. When you think you have to come near to 100% satisfaction stretch your arms high towards the ceiling and bend a little bit backwards to feel more clearly what is going on in your tummy. It's just like having a nice stretch when you are yawning. If doing this feels uncomfortable you have probably eaten too much. Give yourself time to learn to come to 100% satisfaction at each meal and remember that it all boils down to feeling better and better.

Many diet books advise people to stop eating when they are full and then bin any leftovers. If you are like me you don't like throwing food away. It's not because my parents told me that the children in Africa were starving but simply for the reason that I don't like putting something into the rubbish that has so much value for me. If you feel that way too, I recommend that you only put as much food on your plate as you are confident that you can eat. If you want more you can take another helping later on. In this way you can save leftovers and avoid the uncomfortable feeling of having to throw food away. An exception to this rule is obviously eating out in restaurants. Here we have to be tough and leave leftovers on the plate.

Frequently asked questions for enjoyable step four

'I find it hard to notice when I am full.'

The slower you eat, the more thoroughly you chew and the more you pay attention to what is actually happening in your tummy (and not only in your mouth), the easier it will be to notice when you are full. If in doubt, get up from the table, do a few stretches or something else for a few minutes and notice if you still feel hungry. If yes, go back to the table and eat some more.

'I often feel full physically but still somewhat dissatisfied. I may crave a pudding, for example, after having a full meal.'

This can only happen if you didn't allow yourself to eat really yummy food. Most likely, you forced yourself to eat savoury food when you really desired something sweet or you didn't add enough fat or carbohydrates to your meal. Sneaking in some diet food is counter-productive because it will produce food cravings and make it much harder to lose weight. It is much better to eat a pudding and only a pudding if this is what you desire most (and the pudding is prepared with healthy ingredients).

'I find it hard to always fully enjoy my food. Before I know it I have wolfed it down without much mindfulness.'

It might be a good idea to go back to the first exercise in this chapter and try to relish one single bite of food at a time. Do this frequently and you will notice that this new habit will slowly start to creep into your everyday life. Give yourself time and the happy eating approach will make you feel better in every respect. Once you notice this enjoyment you will not want to give it up again.

'Do you recommend taking a multi-vitamin in the happy eating approach?'

There is a lot of talk these days about depleted soils and that our fruit and vegetables don't contain enough minerals and vitamins anymore. However, commercial vitamin preparations have the considerable drawback that they are not easily absorbed into the bloodstream. If you would like to take a multi-vitamin you need to buy vitamins in a 'food-state' from your healthfood shop. Unfortunately, these food-state vitamins are a bit expensive.

A cheaper way of getting lots of high-quality nutrients is to grow your own multi-vitamins in the form of sprouts. Even though these plants are tiny they contain far more vitamins, minerals and enzymes than the full-grown plant. For example, alfalfa sprouts are an abundant source of vitamins A, B, C, E and K along with minerals calcium, iron, magnesium, phosphorus, potassium and zinc. They also contain carotene, chlorophyll, amino acids and trace elements. Alfalfa sprouts taste rather bland on their own which is why they can easily be combined with virtually every meal.

Pitfalls for enjoyable step four

'In the happy eating approach you can overeat as often as you like because your next hunger will be further away and it won't matter.'

This is not true. Overeating puts a strain on our

already stressed digestive organs. Remember, our body is best able to transform food into energy if it is in optimal condition. If not, it is much more likely to store excess calories as fat. Therefore, keeping overeating down to a minimum is paramount in the happy eating approach.

'It's Christmas time and I find it impossible not to overeat.'

There is no need to overeat at any time of the year. Please remember always to ask yourself the question, 'how will this food make me feel after I have eaten it?' You will find that this anticipation of the future will make it much easier to resist overeating. By insisting that you want to feel good before, during and after eating, *you* will be able to make healthy choices even if you are tempted by too many festive foods. Also, remember that it is perfectly viable in the happy eating approach to eat only Christmas pudding and Christmas cake *instead* of a massive three-course meal.

'I'm always the last to finish my meal since I'm following the happy eating approach. I find that embarrassing.'

There are two possibilities for dealing with this situation. First of all, you could humorously encourage the other people to eat just as slowly as you by explaining to them the wonderful health and weight loss benefits. If this is not possible and the embarrassment continues, try not to eat with people who don't support you in your weight loss effort.

'Great, I can snack on my favourite foods whenever I like as long as the physical feeling of hunger goes away each time.'

No, when you feel physically hungry the happy eating approach means having a proper meal so that you get the feeling of being fully satisfied, not just taking the physical feeling of hunger away until the next little snack.

What to do if you fail to follow enjoyable step four

First of all, be kind to yourself and send love to yourself with the help of the exercise at the end of enjoyable step one. The more love you can send to yourself with all your problems and weaknesses, the more quickly you will be able to put your positive resolutions into practice.

If you catch yourself mindlessly stuffing food into your mouth don't be angry with yourself. On the contrary, be happy that you noticed and then focus on your enjoyment. For many people it may take a little while to realise that they really are allowed to enjoy their food – even if they are still overweight. Therefore, no matter how often you fail, simply go back to sitting at a table, chewing slowly and really relishing your food.

If you have eaten too much, try not to worry about

it, either. Simply wait until you are physically hungry again, which will naturally be later than usual. In most cases, this will take care of occasional overeating.

The bottom line for enjoyable step four

Relish every bite of your food.

Eat slowly at a properly laid table and put your fork or spoon down between each bite.

Chew each morsel of your food into a yummy mush.

Notice when you feel 80% satisfied and finish your meal when you are 100% satisfied.

Affirmations for enjoyable step four

The more I truly enjoy my food, the faster I will become slim.

Chewing my food into a thin mush will make me slim.

It feels best to stop eating when I am 100% satisfied.

Enjoyable step five
Love yourself and others

What does loving yourself and others have to do with weight loss? A lot! In fact, a loving attitude is the centrepiece of the happy eating approach and underpins each of the previous four enjoyable steps.

Loving yourself and others basically means wishing yourself and others to be happy. Without this warm wish it is hard, if not impossible, to achieve any positive development anywhere in your life.

Many overweight people don't really love themselves and many even hate themselves for carrying too much weight. Unfortunately, it is this very self-loathing that blocks all attempts to lose weight permanently. So many overweight people say, 'I tried to lose weight many times but I simply can't', and they may blame their genes or some other hidden mechanism in their bodies for their misery. The good news is that the main block is not in their body but in their mind and can easily be unblocked. The key is to go from a self-critical attitude to a self-loving one.

With our self-loathing still in place even the happy eating approach will not work. For example, if we hate ourselves we will not bother to make sure we prepare wholesome food lovingly as described in step two and we will not allow ourselves to really enjoy our food as described in step four. If we are full of self-loathing we will not care if we experience digestive discomfort as described in step three and we will probably still try to starve ourselves brutally, which goes against step one. In other words, we simply wouldn't allow ourselves to experience as much joy and pleasure as is encouraged in the happy eating approach. And this lack of enjoyment will result in eating even more comfort food in quantities that will lead to further weight gain. This in turn will produce guilt-feelings, even more self-loathing and even more overeating.

Simply put, it is almost impossible to change *anything* in our life for the better if we treat ourselves in a self-loathing way. I would like to demonstrate this dynamic with an example that may be a bit upsetting to some people: Imagine a mother of an overweight little boy. Each time the child puts some food in his mouth the mother shouts at him in a degrading and shaming way. 'Somebody as fat as you should be ashamed of eating', she would yell, 'you look like a pig!' You will agree that this would be a very sad and terrible way to treat a child and that it would make it highly unlikely that this child would give up his bad eating habits. Instead, the child would feel sad and confused and would respond with more eating. It is a sad truth that many overweight people talk to themselves in just this horrible way. But hate, anger and criticism only makes matters worse. We all need love to grow and change for the better.

Many overweight people think that they will start to love themselves once they have slimmed

down. But it works exactly the other way round. Once you start to love yourself it will be a whole lot easier to lose weight.

Here is another example that demonstrates this point: Imagine you are married to a very critical person who speaks to you in a harsh and shaming way every time you overeat. Next, imagine you are in a very loving relationship with someone who patiently helps you with all your food problems no matter how often you fall off the wagon. Which relationship will make it more likely that you will lose your weight? I think the answer is obvious.

In order to lose weight the most important relationship is the one we have with ourselves. Ask yourself, 'Am I loving, patient and compassionate towards myself with all my problems and weaknesses?' If you said 'no', 'a bit' or 'partly' to this question, you have discovered your *main obstacle* to a happier and slimmer life. Luckily, this obstacle can be removed quite easily.

How to love yourself

Learning to love yourself is not that difficult. I have taught it to many hundreds of people within a few minutes and once people know how to do it, it is relatively easy to cultivate this warm attitude further and further. In fact, if you have begun using the exercise at the end of enjoyable step one then you have already made a start. Here is a short summary of the exercise again but please revisit the details of this exercise at the end of enjoyable step one once you want to practice it in earnest:

> *Feel the white-golden, loving and healing light in the middle of your chest and let the light radiate throughout your body and around yourself. Join in with this healing light and wish yourself with deepest compassion to be happy and healed from all your problems. Say to yourself, 'I love myself with all my problems and imperfections.'*

As you can see, loving ourselves is not necessarily a strong feeling but starts with compassion for our shortcomings and a *wish* or *intention* for ourselves to be happy and healed. Without this wish we can never overcome our problems and we can never lose weight permanently. It seems like a very obvious thing to say but many people find loving themselves difficult until they are shown this step-by-step approach. But once they have learnt how to do it, it becomes quite doable.

Loving ourselves with all our problems and weaknesses does not require *liking* our excess fat. However, it is very important not to hate or loathe our body anymore. Stopping this self-loathing is not that difficult. There is only room for one thought or emotion in our mind and if we focus wholeheartedly on the loving light within and around ourselves while repeating the sentences mentioned above, we eradicate all our self-loathing even if we still carry excess weight. As soon as our self-critical thoughts and feelings arise, we simply shift our mind back to our loving thoughts and visualisation. We may have to repeat this shift many times over but with time we will get more familiar with our newly found love and compassion for ourselves and this attitude will become more and more automatic.

The aim is to become our own best friend. A true friend wouldn't constantly focus on our shortcomings but see the good and the beautiful in us. Even if we dislike certain parts of our body (and character) we can still love ourselves as a whole person and very kindly wish for ourselves that we overcome our problems. In other words, we need to be compassionate with ourselves *with* all our shortcomings and imperfections.

Making these loving wishes for ourselves is not that difficult but in order to get rid of all our self-loathing we need to do it daily, if not hourly. The negative attitudes that we have towards ourselves are often semi-conscious and if we don't consciously replace them with love every single day they often creep back very quickly. Eventually, we will be able to send love to ourselves whenever we feel a negative feeling around any food or body issue without having to sit down and concentrate hard on these thoughts and images.

If you frequently practice loving yourself, you will find that your self-loathing will gradually be replaced with a much friendlier attitude. Whenever you notice any negative thoughts and feelings around your weight *immediately* go back to your inner light and send compassionate love to yourself. It is very important never to allow yourself to let destructive self-criticism fester within you for any length of time. The following quote comes from one of my clients and he speaks for many others who all say virtually the same:

> *I find the loving light in my heart very helpful and comforting. It gives you something positive to focus on whenever negative feelings come up or when you are tempted to eat without hunger. The crucial point is to notice your negative thoughts earlier and earlier and not to listen to them. Instead, you put your mind on your inner light and let it radiate out with love. That is wonderfully healing and I have noticed that my negative thoughts and feelings have become less and less.*

Being happy now

When you start to love yourself and nourish this positive attitude with daily practice something wonderful will happen – you will become happier despite all your imperfections and despite all the excess weight that you may still carry around. Many of my clients noted that this positive development came to them as a big surprise. Like many overweight people they thought that they had to wait until they were slim before they could be happy. But once they embarked in earnest on the happy eating approach they noticed that happiness was almost an effortless side-effect of it. Let me say it more dramatically:

Happiness doesn't come from being slim. It comes from loving ourselves and others.

Most of us have read stories about beautiful actresses and models who felt painfully self-conscious about their body even though the whole world thought that they were nearly perfect. In my counselling practice I have also worked with quite a number of women who were very good-looking but were constantly worried about their appearance. On the other hand, I have known many average looking or slightly overweight people who had none of these worries. The reason for these seemingly paradoxical attitudes is that our sense of beauty is directly linked to how much we can love ourselves. Simply put:

If we love ourselves, we feel beautiful no matter what the rest of the world is thinking. If we don't love ourselves, we perceive ourselves as ugly even if we are the most highly paid model.

Therefore, learning to love ourselves on a daily basis is the most important condition for success in the happy eating approach. Once we love ourselves, we will be happier. And once we are happier we will be better at everything we do. We will be better parents, we will be better at doing our work and we will be better at losing weight.

Sometimes my clients complain that loving themselves is 'too much like hard work' but I don't agree. Focusing on your inner light as described above is pure pleasure – there is nothing hard about it. Just like the happy eating approach, the point is to notice the pleasure and to stick with it.

How to make the mirror friendlier

Did you notice that there must be something wrong with mirrors? One day they show us an acceptable or even good-looking reflection and yet the next day we look like a monster in the same mirror. How is this possible? The answer is that *nobody* sees their mirror reflection as it really is. We either beautify what we see or we uglify it. We can't help it – it is the same mechanism that makes our life look very positive one day and very negative the next in an exaggerated way that bears little resemblance to reality. Unfortunately, our mind is rather incapable at seeing things as they are but always has a tendency to add on an extra layer of beautifying or uglifying interpretation.

If you like, you can try this out for yourself and do the following exercise that I also offer in my happy eating approach groups. You need a large sheet of paper that is as big as your whole body. First you draw your life-size body contours on the paper as you remember them from your reflection in the mirror. For the second step you need a friend. You lie down in the middle of what you thought your body contours look like and let your friend draw the real contours around your body. You will probably be positively surprised at how much slimmer the real you is in comparison with your inner self-image.

Most overweight people see themselves bigger than they really are. Doing a reality check as in the exercise above can be a healing revelation. However, there are also some obese people who see themselves as much slimmer than they actually are. You are probably not one of them simply because those people usually don't want to do anything about their weight. They really don't see the need for it. Having this laid-back attitude may seem enviable at first sight but it is actually a bit dangerous because it keeps them from taking the necessary action when their weight is putting their health at risk. The ideal is to see ourselves just as we are, be compassionate with our shortcomings and then take skilful action to overcome these shortcomings.

In order to deal with the mirror in an empowering way we need to understand that the beautifying or uglifying process only starts after a few moments of looking at our appearance. In the first few moments we can see ourselves as we really are without making ourselves better or worse through our fantasy. After that, most people hone in on what's wrong with them and then exaggerate any perceived weakness, for example, they see a slightly crooked nose as very crooked or a slightly plump figure as extremely fat.

If you want, you can find out if this applies to you, as well. Stand in front of your mirror with closed eyes and then open your eyes. Pay very sharp attention to how long it takes until you hone in on your weak points and start telling yourself how 'ugly' and 'terrible' they are. For some people this process may take no longer than one second while others may be able to look in the mirror for a half a minute, perhaps even three minutes, before they start fixating on their faults. The time span *before* the uglifying process starts is your personal 'positive mirror time'. No matter how long your positive mirror time is, you are inviting 'trouble' if you try to look at yourself for longer than this time span.

The good news is that sending love to yourself as explained in the previous section may extend your positive mirror time if you practice diligently. However, it is important to be patient with this process and not to expect that your mirror experience will change overnight. The basic tendency of our mind to always hone in on 'what's wrong' will probably limit the positive mirror time even in the most confident and self-loving individuals. This does not need to be a big problem because loving oneself is not meant to teach people to become narcissistic and vain. At the end of the day, what really matters is that we feel happy and compassionate with ourselves and others.

If you understand these dynamics you can stop wondering why it doesn't work to look in the mirror and repeat for hours 'I am beautiful; I am beautiful; I am beautiful …'. Instead, you can send love to yourself and stay within the limits of your personal 'positive mirror time'. In this way you will be satisfied every time you look at yourself.

I once read an article about a gorgeous model who employed exactly the same technique. The model said, 'I look in the mirror and go. I don't wait until I come to the point when I start dissecting myself as I did in the past. One glance is enough and then I go.'

The words of this model are just another proof that objective beauty and a personal feeling of being beautiful have not much to do with each other. One would have thought that any model could indulge in their own beauty for hours on end but this is certainly not the case. As the saying goes, 'beauty is in the eye of the beholder' and it is largely determined by how much we genuinely love who we see.

How to deal with the scales in an empowering way

Bathroom scales were not invented as instruments of torture but unfortunately they are exactly that in many people's lives. If you feel tortured by the scales and your day is ruined each time the scales are not showing your desired weight there is only one thing to do – take the horrible thing and throw it into the rubbish bin with relish. End of story. There's nothing more to say.

I strongly recommend that you do the same with all the tiny clothes that you keep in your wardrobe for the time you have lost weight – or at least banish them into the corner of your loft that is most difficult to reach. Keeping clothes in your wardrobe that are too small for you will do nothing for your self-confidence because they are constant reminders that you have 'failed'. We don't need these negative reminders if we are learning to a have a more loving relationship with ourselves – therefore throw everything out that makes you feel like a failure.

Some of my clients only allow themselves to go shopping for clothes once they have lost weight with the result that almost everything in their wardrobe is too small. It is of paramount importance that you allow yourself to have the most beautiful and comfortable clothes you can find – *now* – and that they are the only ones that you keep in your wardrobe. Remember, everything changes best in the light of love. Allowing ourselves to feel good in our clothes is an act of love for ourselves and once we feel loved we will be more successful with the happy eating approach.

If you find that the scales don't make you feel bad, then and only then can it be a useful instrument to give you feedback on your weight loss. Most people find it easier to lose weight on the happy eating approach if they have a reliable way of getting feedback on their progress. In this way they get encouragement when they are doing well and an early warning if they are not keeping properly to the guidelines of the happy eating approach.

Generally speaking, the more information we have about a certain topic the easier it is to manage and change it for the better. Examples are how we deal with our teeth or finances. It is common knowledge that having regular check-ups with a dentist makes it easier to prevent major problems with our teeth. Similarly, writing down all our expenses will make it much easier to find the areas where we inadvertently overspend and then change this negative trend. The same is true for our weight-management: the more information we have about this topic, the easier it will be to see where we inadvertently overeat and change the pattern for the better.

Unfortunately, most ordinary bathroom scales are very unreliable. You can easily see this unreliability by weighing yourself ten times in a row. Most scales will throw up many different weights, which may vary by up to several pounds. It is obvious that this kind of 'feedback' on our weight loss endeavour is near to useless. To make matters worse, our own weight also fluctuates up to several pounds a day due to water retention, which may be severe if we have food allergies or eat too much salt on a particular day.

The common advice is to weigh yourself only once a week and not every day so that you won't get too upset about these variations. But I do not agree with this approach because you could get a very high and incorrect reading on your weighing day, which will be confusing and disheartening when you have actually felt good with yourself on the happy eating approach. A much more precise way of finding your correct weight is to weigh yourself every day for a week and then calculate the average of those seven days by adding up all seven weights and dividing them by seven. This average counts as the weight for that week. Using this approach has two advantages as it takes care of the unreliability of the scale and of your own weight fluctuations, as well.

If you would like to get an even more accurate picture of your actual weight and which foods cause your sudden weight gain through water retention, you should consider investing in a 'calibrated scale'. This is one of those scales that you would find in your doctor's surgery, for example from the Seca company. These scales are actually able to measure your weight down to 50 grams. They are a bit expensive but it can make weight loss a lot easier simply because they give us better data and therefore more precise feedback on what is actually happening to our weight when we eat certain foods.

Other ways of keeping track of your size and weight are using a fat caliper or a body tape measure. This requires buying small gadgets that you can easily find on the internet but both these methods are far less reliable ways of measuring yourself compared with a calibrated scale.

In summary, one can say that we need to extend our mindfulness practice to keep track of our actual size and weight. The more precise information we can get about ourselves the easier it will be to achieve our weight loss goal.

The power of imagination for weight loss

Once I had a client who was so depressed about her weight gain that she couldn't go to work. When I asked her about the details it turned out that she had gone from being very slim to being grossly obese within a year. She worked in public relations and for her job it was quite important to come across as fit and attractive. This was indeed an unusual development and I quizzed my client about how this rapid weight gain had come about. My client was very reluctant to tell me the truth but eventually she admitted that she had had liposuction surgery. Before the operation she had been slightly overweight but after the procedure her weight had just shot up and seemed unstoppable. Why do you think this happened?

This example shows that the power of our mind is far more important for our weight loss success than any diet or even a drastic measure like liposuction. Despite getting a dream figure from her operation my client still 'saw' herself as fat and this was exactly what manifested shortly afterwards in her disastrous development. Our imagination is powerful and if we really understand this truth we can use it to manifest a slim body.

You may have already heard that it is possible to 'visualise yourself slim'. Many people scoff at this idea because they do not believe that this can work. In some respects they are right because these techniques will definitely not work so long as our self-loathing is still active. In order for visualisations to actually manifest, we need *first* to give up any form of self-aversion and love ourselves instead, as we have already discussed. But once we have learnt to love ourselves our imagination can bring almost miraculous results. Why is this so?

The answer is simple: under the influence of hatred or strong dislike everything becomes rigid and resistant; under the influence of love everything becomes willing and able to change for the better. Remember the poor overweight boy with his angry mother. As long as the mother continues to say, 'You are fat. You are fat. You are fat.' it will be virtually impossible for the child to change. But if a loving parent continuously says, 'You are getting slimmer every day. I can see the slim, fit and muscular boy already within you', it is much more likely that the boy will achieve his aim.

It is the same with us. First, we need to give up our negative attitude towards ourselves and only then is visualising ourselves slim likely to have a strong effect. The following exercise will show you how to use the power of visualisation to achieve your weight loss goal.

Visualising yourself slim

Find a *picture of a person with the kind of body you would like to have (from a clothes catalogue, for example, or of yourself when you were slim), and replace the head with a photo of your own up-to-date head. Stick (or Photoshop) everything together in a credible way.*

Look at *this picture and vividly imagine that this is a picture of the new you. Then close your eyes and imagine being **in** the beautiful body of your collage.*

Feel *the happiness that arises from having the body of your dreams. The stronger your positive feelings the more successful you will be with*

> *these kinds of exercises.*
>
> ***Hear in*** *your mind how people are complimenting you on your great body.*
>
> ***Focus on these*** *inner images and emotions for 5 to 10 minutes (or as long as you have time) each day after you have given yourself love in the exercise that we discussed earlier.*

There is nothing weird about using these techniques. They are widely used in sales and all successful sports people work with visualisation, too. They also try their hardest not to indulge in any negative images of losing. It is actually highly unlikely these days to find someone winning a top sports competition who doesn't do these visualisation exercises because all their competitors are doing these kinds of mental exercises, as well. This is the reason why over the years people have become able to run faster, jump higher and move in ever more sophisticated ways. The human body hasn't improved – this positive development happened because the sports world discovered the power of imagination.

You can employ exactly the same method and if you frequently visualise yourself with a slim body you can't fail to develop a new sense of your ideal self. The key point is repetition. No matter how long it takes to achieve your perfect body, simply keep visualising and feeling that you are slim until this new body has manifested.

From now on, *never* allow yourself to indulge in

self-loathing about your excess fat.

Keep strictly within the limit of your positive mirror time so that you are not tempted to hone in on your flaws. By the same token, only ever wear clothes wide enough such that they don't make you feel fat. The more loving and positive thoughts and feelings you have about your body and your food, the easier it will be to lose weight.

The affirmations that I have provided at the end of each chapter can help you to keep your positive visualisation going. However, please only use those affirmations that you find easy to believe and avoid creating an inner war through trying to 'hammer them into your head' when you find them hard to accept. If this happens, it is much more effective to visualise the loving healing light in the middle of your chest and then surround yourself with this light in order to cut through any negative thoughts and feelings. You can also use these techniques if you suffer from excessively worrying that the happy eating approach might not work for you.

Visualisation techniques always need to go together with action in the real world. One without the other will not bring you very far but as a package this approach is hard to beat. An athlete, for instance, needs to visualise *and* to train and, in the same way, we need to visualise ourselves slim *and* keep to the steps of the happy eating approach.

The power of imagination is very strong and I myself use it in every area of my life. Professional success, emotional well-being and relationships – I would never leave any of these areas to chance.

Instead, I consciously steer my life so that all my dreams are fulfilled. If you would like to read more about how to make your wishes come true, please refer to my book *Advanced Manifesting*.

Loving others

You may find it hard to believe but many overweight people have in their unconscious mind a strong psychological reason for staying fat. These invisible obstacles are usually created through unhealthy relationships with other people. The good news is that these blocks can only ever have a hold on people so long as they stay unconscious. As soon as people become aware of them, they start losing their power. In order to make people conscious of these hidden obstacles I lead them through the so-called 'miracle exercise'.

In a few moments I will introduce you to this exercise so that you can find out if you yourself have a hidden psychological obstacle to losing weight. But first I want to share with you some typical insights that my clients came up with over the years after doing this exercise so that you know what kind of things to expect. Barbara said:

> *When Tara did the miracle exercise with me I suddenly realised that getting slim would create severe problems in the relationship with my sister who means the world to me. She is grossly overweight, far more than I am, and she has many other problems, as well. I felt*

> *that if I became slim it would be unkind to her because my life has always been better than hers and if I now would even succeed at being slim it would make her very depressed.*

Mary said:

> *If I succeeded in having a slim body I feel that my friends would judge me as selfish and materialistic. I don't want to be seen in that way.*

Martha said:

> *I am shocked by what I have discovered. I think if I am slim I would leave my husband. Staying fat is like an insurance policy for our marriage because it makes me grateful that at least I have found someone.*

Harriet said:

> *I work as business consultant - mostly with men. If I would be slim I would feel very vulnerable in this environment because the men would start to see me as a sex-object. I couldn't cope with that. Being fat makes sure that none of them thinks of sleeping with me when we work together.*

Hannah said:

> *If I became slim I fear that people would be more interested in my body than in my mind. I am afraid that the 'real me'*

would be less interesting for people.

Katie said:

> *If I became slim and good-looking I fear that I couldn't stop myself from having a lot of casual sex. I find that frightening and staying overweight makes sure I am not confident enough to do such a thing. Also, I am less attractive and many men wouldn't want to sleep with me, anyway.*

Sandy said:

> *I discovered that being really slim evoked a strong fear that other people would be envious. In my mind I saw people around me with hateful eyes trying to hurt me because I had what they didn't.*

Robert said:

> *I noticed that overeating was a way of keeping my anger under control. Women sometimes tell me that I am like a cuddly teddy bear who they can trust and feel safe with. When I did the miracle exercise I suddenly noticed how much more aggressive and dominant I saw myself with a slim body. No more cuddly teddy bear! I find that actually quite disconcerting.*

All these people were completely unconscious about the powerful obstacles that would sabotage their efforts to lose weight from an unconscious level, no matter which diet they tried. Unfortunately, as long as these beliefs stay unconscious they can't be dealt with efficiently. Once they have become conscious they can be dealt with in a quick and straightforward way. I will tell you now how it can be done:

Each and every unconscious psychological obstacle to weight loss can be removed and overcome by sending love to it. I instructed Barbara, for example, to send love to her disadvantaged sister and to ponder the question whether it would really help her sister if she stayed fat for her sister's sake. It took two weeks before Barbara had freed herself from her main psychological obstacle to weight loss and then she easily lost most of her excess weight and is now within several pounds of her goal-weight. All the other people from above were instructed, as well, to send love to the people (real or imagined) who were making them feel that it was 'safer' to stay fat. Doing this had very positive results for all of them. Katie, for example, who feared that she would have lots of casual sex if she lost her weight, said:

> *I've sent love to all the guys I could possibly imagine having sex with and to my surprise I discovered that my desire either diminished or that I was more interested in having a 'proper' relationship with them. This whole issue of being afraid of my uncontrollable sexual appetite dissolved into thin air.*

And another client told me:

> *I was very fat as a child and my father always told me off in a degrading way. I felt very hurt by his attitude and still did until recently. I discovered through the miracle exercise that losing weight would make me feel as if I had given in to my father and I didn't want that. Staying fat was my way of saying to my father, 'go away with all your criticism – I do what I want and I am not becoming slim only to please you.'*
>
> *Obviously, all this is very counter-productive. Once I started to send love to my father this whole psychological trap disappeared. I started to phone my father and I now feel fond of him for the first time in many years. My weight loss that had stagnated has now taken off again.*

Are you ready to find out if you yourself have any unconscious obstacles to losing weight? The following exercise has proven very effective and you need approximately ten minutes of undisturbed quiet time to do it.

The miracle exercise

Relax *for a few moments.*

Imagine *that you wake up one day and a miracle has happened. As you get out of bed you find that* *you now have your dream figure. You are absolutely perfect and you look like you always wanted to look.*

Now you *go to a body-size mirror and you look at yourself from all sides. How do you feel? Probably, you will feel very happy but I want you to also pay special attention to any negative feelings that you may have (for example nervousness, anxiety, lack of joy or guilt). Even if these negative feelings are very shadowy and hardly noticeable under the upsurge of joy, make a mental note of anything negative you may experience.*

When you *get dressed you find that your wardrobe is full of well-fitting, beautiful clothes. Choose something you like and again notice if there are any negative thoughts or feelings creeping in.*

When you *leave your bedroom you meet the people you live with. Of course, they'll immediately notice the wonderful change in your appearance. What do they say and how do you feel? Do you experience even the slightest negative feeling?*

Now you *go about your daily business and meet the people that you usually meet. Again, notice if your new appearance makes you feel uncomfortable in any way.*

Later that *day, there is a big family meeting. All your relatives are there and notice your new figure. How do you feel? Anything negative?*

In the evening *there is a big party where you meet all your friends and lots of other sexually attractive people of your own age. How do you dress, how do you relate to the other people and how do you feel? Is there any shadowy feeling that makes you feel uncomfortable?*

If there *is anybody in your life who is important to you and you haven't met by now, meet this person now and as before notice if you feel any negative feelings, no matter how small.*

Open your *eyes and write down any negative feelings that you experienced and to which person each one is connected. This may be someone you know or an anonymous mass of people like, 'when I entered the party it felt like everyone was staring at me. That made me feel a bit uncomfortable'. If you found any negative feeling rejoice because you can now start to remove this obstacle to your weight loss.*

Imagine your *white-golden sun in the middle of your chest underneath the breastbone radiating light throughout your body and all around it. It is a healing and loving light that brings comfort to all of your problems. Wish yourself to be happy and healed.*

Now imagine *that the person(s) who caused you concern are also penetrated and surrounded by loving light just like you. Wish these people to be happy with all your heart. If someone has hurt you, state the reasons for your pain clearly and then wish this person to be happy and healed. Remember, everybody changes best in the light of*

> *love and would immediately repent all their wrong-doing. Do this for two minutes twice a day until your negative feeling has dissolved.*

The power of love to remove and resolve our problems is truly amazing. If you would like to learn more about the healing power of love, please have a look at my book *The Five-Minute Miracle*.

Frequently asked questions for enjoyable step five

'I did the miracle exercise but I couldn't find any negative feelings.'

Good for you. In that case, just concentrate on sending love to yourself and stick to the four other enjoyable steps of the happy eating approach as well as you can. However, if you find yourself frequently overeating junk food despite your best intentions, you may still have some unaddressed psychological issues. Go through the miracle exercise a few more times and try to admit even the tiniest negative feeling to yourself. Alternatively, send love to everyone in your personal surroundings, to every person who was important to you in the past and finally to the whole world. In this way you should have covered all possible psychological obstacles that you haven't dealt with consciously.

'How often should I visualise myself slim?'

The short answer is – all the time. The long answer is – work with the loving light in your heart and with your visualisation techniques for five minutes twice a day until you have reached your goal-figure and you feel secure with your new slim figure. During your everyday activities try to catch yourself in the act when you succumb to self-loathing or negative thinking and immediately go back to sending love to yourself. Keep doing this until your negative feelings subside.

Pitfalls for enjoyable step five

'I agree with step one to four of the happy eating approach but step five is just psychological mumbo-jumbo'.

Don't be too sure! This so-called psychological mumbo-jumbo is actually the most important step of all. Why do so many people fail to lose weight even though the advice of the happy eating approach is really common sense? It is their unresolved psychological issues, their bad self-image and a deep belief that it is impossible to lose weight. If you want to belong to the people who are successful with their weight loss long-term, you would be well-advised to work on your mind *as well* as on your body.

'I just can't love myself as long as I am fat.'

Love is not so much a feeling as it is a wish – the

wish for yourself to be happy. Imagine you had a child who was less than perfect (as all children are). You could still love this child and wish her to be happy, couldn't you? In the same way you can wish yourself to be happy even though you are not perfect.

'I discovered something during the miracle exercise that I find hard to forgive.'

When you send love to someone who has hurt you, you don't condone what they have done. Instead, you wish them to be happy because a happy person would immediately repent everything negative they have done and apologise. Happy people are loving people, which is why wishing people to be happy is such a healing thing to do.

What to do if you fail to follow enjoyable step five

First of all, be kind to yourself and send love to yourself with all your problems and imperfections. The more love you can send to yourself, the more quickly you will see results in the happy eating approach.

You are bound to catch yourself experiencing self-loathing, looking critically in the mirror, avoiding measuring your weight or size, or generally being trapped in your old psychological pitfalls again. Instead of adding insult to injury by getting even angrier with yourself, simply send love to yourself and gently correct your ways. We have to be patient with ourselves just as parents have to be patient with their children. Constant yelling at children only results in them becoming deaf and constant self-loathing only results in us being defiant and eating even more. There is a way out of this dilemma and that is the insistence on enjoying our food and loving ourselves and others.

The bottom line for enjoyable step five

Learn to love yourself with all your weaknesses and problems. Respond to your physical imperfections and your problems around food with self-compassion rather than with self-criticism.

Recognise your 'positive mirror-time' and stay within that limit.

Find a way to get accurate feedback on your size and weight that works for you - either with scales, body tape or a fat caliper.

Visualise yourself slim.

Cut through self-loathing, negative thinking and worrying by immediately going back to the loving light in your heart and your kind wishes for yourself.

Find out if you have any hidden psychological obstacles to weight loss and send love to the very people who make it difficult for you to lose weight.

Affirmations for enjoyable step five

I love myself with all my weaknesses and problems.

I can see myself slim and beautiful.

I wish everybody who makes me uncomfortable when I am slim to be happy and healed.

Sample page for a food diary

Time / date of meal or snack and what I ate:

Was I physically hungry? (yes) (no)
Insights:

Did I choose natural foods? (yes) (no)
Insights:

Did I choose food that I really liked and that I thought would agree with me? (yes) (no)
Insights:

Did I chew slowly, relish the food and stop when I was 100% satisfied? (yes) (no)
Insights:

Did I send love to myself when I had negative thoughts and feelings? (yes) (no)
Insights:

Was there any food that didn't agree with me? (yes) (no) Insights:

About the author

From teenage years onwards Tara has been deeply interested in personal growth and self-development and has dedicated her life to this quest.

Tara holds an M.A. in Education and has post-graduate qualifications in gestalt therapy, body awareness therapy and transpersonal therapy. She is a fully qualified and licensed psychotherapist and counsellor. Tara has worked as a drugs counsellor, counsellor for adolescents and general psychotherapist since 1988.

Tara has successfully helped many clients suffering from a negative body image, eating disorders and weight loss problems both in groups and one-to-one.

Tara has been a dedicated Buddhist practitioner since 1986. In 1997 she received encouragement from her Buddhist teacher Rigdzin Shikpo to teach meditation to others. In 2002 her Buddhist teacher Venerable Garchen Rinpoche also encouraged her to teach.

Tara has since taught on-going meditation groups and combines Buddhist wisdom and her experience in counselling when assisting her clients with their personal growth, self development and improvement.

Tara is the author of several self-help books. She has been featured in numerous publications and has appeared on various radio and television shows in Europe and the US.

Tara can be contacted via her website at www.taraspringett.com or directly via tara@taraspringett.com

Printed in Great Britain
by Amazon